Care and Conservation of Collections

A Bibliography on
Historical Organization Practices

Care and Conservation of Collections

Compiled by
Rosemary S. Reese

Edited by

Frederick L. Rath, Jr.
and
Merrilyn Rogers O'Connell

American Association for State and Local History
Nashville, Tennessee

We are grateful for the generous support of the American Conservation Association, Inc. for their assistance in the publication of this volume.

Publication of this book was made possible in part by funds from the sale of the Bicentennial State Histories.

Library of Congress Cataloging in Publication Data (Revised)

Rath, Frederick L
  A bibliography on historical organization practices.

  Includes index.
  CONTENTS: v. 1. Historic preservation.—v. 2. Care and conservation of collections, compiled by R. S. Reese.
  1. Historic buildings—United States—Conservation and restoration—Bibliography.   2. Historic Sites—United States—Conservation and restoration—Bibliography.
3. Historic buildings—Conservation and restoration—Bibliography.   4. Historical museums—Bibliography.
5. Museum techniques—Bibliography.   I. O'Connell, Merrilyn Rogers, joint author.   II. Title.
Z1251.A2R35   016.069′53   75–26770

Printed in the United States of America

Contents

Preface

The second volume of *A Bibliography on Historical Organization Practices* turns to the frequently unglamorous but always necessary care of priceless collections—the paintings, documents, books, photographs, and other artifacts—without which there would be no exhibits, no research, no educational programs, no interpretation.

Unhappily, for too long there has been little consciousness that all collections are prey to the ravages of time and environment and, even more important, the handling by man, their greatest enemy. Poor storage conditions; harmful lighting; careless, uninformed, and unscientific handling have taken an irrevocable toll in too many museums and historical societies in the world today. In recent years, however, more and more agencies, organizations, and individuals, alerted to the disastrous effects of inattention, have begun to build into their historical and artistic-resource management programs provisions for maintenance of collections. It is conscious, planned maintenance—the careful expenditure of energy on daily "little things"—that can produce effective, long-term preservation at minimal cost. Eventually it obviates the need for the kind of expensive conservation treatment that is necessitated by neglect.

This volume has been compiled to assist two groups of people. Trustees, administrators, curators and others concerned with the continued well-being of their collections will find the first five chapters particularly helpful. In addition, there are some general references in the last four chapters which will be useful to the nonspecialist. Professional conservators will, hopefully, find the entire volume valuable. In the last four chapters, in particular, there are many references to highly technical publications which they may need to consult.

This bibliography, like the editions which preceded it, is selective rather than definitive. It seeks to include all the most significant references, but some older materials, particularly periodical literature, and some superseded materials have been dropped in order to accommodate the burgeoning new literature. The compilers, aided by their expert advisors, have also exercised an arbitrary discretion in not listing articles in obscure or unattainable editions or periodicals. Although some early seminal or definitive references are still included, the concentration is on books and pamphlets, and articles published since 1945.

As in the second edition, all entries for books and pamphlets follow the Library of Congress main headings and have additional data based on the Library of Congress catalog card information. Thus, all include the following: number of pages or number of volumes; illustrations (if any), including drawings, plans, photographs, or other graphic materials; bibliography or bibliographical footnotes (if any); and the designation "paper" or "mimeo" wherever the entry is not a hard-cover publication.

The primary purpose of the bibliography is to be a working tool, providing the first steps on research trails. To add to its practicality, the compilers have included annotations where the title of the book or article does not give a clear idea of subject matter.

They have included filmed or taped materials where appropriate. At the end of many chapters there are notes on periodicals, organizations or services. The appendix lists all periodicals from which articles have been cited, with addresses and subscription information. The index, derived from a punchcard retrieval system, is deliberately comprehensive, so that the most obscure references, coauthors, editors, or even allusions can be tracked down easily.

There are two other departures from what may be considered standard bibliographical practice which give further dimension to the usefulness of the work. A Basic Reference Shelf, thoroughly annotated, is offered in order to give immediate practical guidance on many facets of collections care and conservation. There is also a discursive section on major conservation organizations, national, foreign, and international.

The compilers wish to acknowledge the fact that bibliographies are outdated as quickly as they are "finished." However, it is hoped that this volume will provide curators and conservators with a useful data base of references. Organization headquarters and editorial offices do tend to change as officers change, and sources for keeping up with new addresses are noted in the Appendix. A few important new publications and address changes, specifically brought to our attention, have been included where possible at press time.

To produce a bibliography of this kind, the help of many individuals and organizations is necessary. Rosemary S. Reese, Associate Editor of the Bibliographic Project, served as principal compiler of this volume *Care and Conservation of Collections*. The Smithsonian Institution, as administrator of National Museum Act funds, made the expanded Bibliographic Project possible. We are especially grateful to the Advisory Council and to Paul N. Perrot. The New York State Historical Association provided not only rooms for the small staff but also the full services of its fine library. The resources of the Conservation of Historic and Artistic Works, Cooperstown Graduate Programs, were especially helpful.

In compiling this volume, we gratefully acknowledge the invaluable guidance, constructive criticism, and insistence on quality from Per Guldbeck, Carolyn Horton, Sheldon Keck, and José Oracca who assisted with many specialized sections.

As we noted in the first volume on *Historic Preservation*, the American Association for State and Local History undertook the support of the Bibliographic Project in recognition that this growing profession must have a reference guide to the myriad of books and articles that are defining and refining the field. We are indebted to Dr. William T. Alderson for his continuing guidance in this effort; and to the Association's publications department, under the direction of Gary G. Gore, without which there would have been no finished product.

Finally, we are grateful to the American Conservation Association, Inc. for partial support of the publication of this and subsequent volumes in this series. Additional publication support came from sales of the Bicentennial State Histories series.

And so, as we have said in earlier volumes, happy hunting.

Frederick L. Rath, Jr.
Deputy Commissioner for Historic Preservation,
New York State Office of Parks and Recreation

Merrilyn Rogers O'Connell
Director, Bibliographic Project

A Bibliography on Historical
Organization Practices

Care and Conservation of Collections

Basic Reference Shelf

The Basic Reference Shelf includes volumes, booklets and reprinted articles that should be part of the working library of every organization and individual involved in the care of collections. Most references contain important bibliographies or are bibliographies in a specialized area, which will provide leads to other sources. The selections fall into two main categories: technical references for the professional conservator, and general references for the curator or others responsible for preventive maintenance. This distinction is indicated in the annotations for each entry.

Clapp, Anne F. *Curatorial Care of Works of Art on Paper.* Oberlin, Ohio: Intermuseum Conservation Association, 1973. 105 pp., list of suppliers, bibliog., paperback. ◆ Includes discussions of factors potentially harmful to paper, various procedures in the care of works of art on paper, equipment and materials of the workroom and storage areas and a list of supplies and sources.

Conference on the Conservation of Textiles, Delft, 1964. Collected Preprints. 2nd ed. London: International Institute for Conservation, 1964. 153 pp., illus., charts, tables. ◆ Technical, a useful reference for the conservator. Includes biodeterioration of textiles and its prevention; cleaning, repair and renovation; color fading and fixation; education of restorers.

The Conservation of Cultural Property with Special Reference to Tropical Conditions. Museums and Monuments, XI. Paris: UNESCO, 1968. 341 pp., photos, drawings, diagrams, tables, maps, formulae, appendices, bibliog., index. ◆ Articles by experts in the field on climate and microclimate, moulds, insects, conservation of glass, stone, metals, textiles, leather, wood, archival materials and paintings; recommendations on lighting, air conditioning, storage and handling. Very technical but an excellent reference on the problems of conservation in the tropics.

Dudley, Dorothy H., and Irma B. Wilkinson, et al. *Museum Registration Methods.* Rev. ed. Washington, D.C.: American Association of Museums, 1968. 294 pp., illus., forms, plans, bibliog., index. ◆ Covers aspects of storage, packing, registration, classification and inspection of art objects and includes a trial glossary for describing condition. Revised edition in progress.

Gettens, Rutherford J., and George L. Stout. *Painting Materials: A Short Encyclopedia.* 1942. Reprint. New York: Dover Publications, 1966. 333 pp., illus., bibliog., glossary, paperback. ◆ A reliable source of information on materials used as supports, grounds, pigments, media, adhesives, varnishes and solvents and on equipment and tools, in painting past and present. A valuable reference for professional conservators and research scholars.

Guldbeck, Per E. *The Care of Historical Collections: A Conservation Handbook for the Non-Specialist.* Rev. ed. Nashville, Tenn.: American Association for State and Local History, 1972. 160 pp., photos, drawings, diagrams, tables, bibliog., supply list, appendices, paperback. ◆ Provides an introduction to the problems of conservation and describes basic procedures for the care of museum collections. Includes advice on the treatment of paper, wood, leather, textiles, ceramics and related materials. Deals with the environmental aspects of conservation, documentation of artifacts, and the equipment of a conservation laboratory. Intended as a practical manual for the small historical society.

Harvard University, William Hayes Fogg Art Museum. *Technical Studies in the Field of the Fine Arts.* Cambridge, Mass.: Harvard University Press, 1932–1942. 10 vols. ◆ An invaluable source of information on materials, techniques, environmental control, technical examination and conservation and restoration procedures. This pioneer work has been reprinted in photo-facsimile with a cumulative index. Available from: Garland Publishing, Inc., 10 East 44th Street, New York, New York 10017. It is very expensive however, and should probably be considered for purchase by libraries rather than individuals.

Horton, Carolyn. *Cleaning and Preserving Bindings and Related Materials.* 2nd ed., rev. Chicago: Library Technology Project, American Library Association, 1969. 87 pp., illus., bibliog., paperback. ◆ Includes information on reconditioning a library, sorting books and identifying problems and treatment of worn and damaged books; list of supplies and equipment, sources of supply and a glossary. This helpful and clearly written book provides much practical advice to the novice.

International Institute for Conservation of Historic and Artistic Works. *Conservation of Stone. Vol. I. Preprints of the Contributions to the New York Conference on Conservation of Stone and Wooden Objects, June 7–13, 1970.* 2nd ed., rev. London: The Institute, 1971. 134 pp., illus., charts, diagrams, references. ◆ Technical, a useful reference for the conservator. Includes articles on decay of stone, impregnation, removal of soluble salts, mud brick preservation, stabilization of adobe and stone and deterioration of sculptural stone.

International Institute for Conservation of Historic and Artistic Works. *Conservation of Wooden Objects. Vol. II. Preprints of the Contributions to the New York Conference on Conservation of Stone and Wooden Objects, June 7–13, 1970.* 2nd ed. London: The Institute, 1971. 140 pp., illus., diagrams, graphs, charts, bibliog. ◆ Technical, a useful reference for the conservator. Includes articles on deterioration of wood and its prevention, consolidation, dimensional stabilization, freeze-drying and insect damage.

Keck, Caroline K. *A Handbook on the Care of Paintings.* Rev. ed. Nashville, Tenn.: American Association for State and Local History, 1967. 136 pp., photos, tables, sources of supply, glossary, bibliog., index, paperback. ◆ Contains basic information on the precautions to be taken for the conservation of paintings. Includes descriptions of the physical structure of paintings, the techniques of laboratory examination and treatment performed by conservators, and a discussion of conservation priorities and procedures. Intended as practical instruction for curators and custodians not as a manual of conservation techniques.

Keck, Caroline K. *Safeguarding Your Collection in Travel.* Nashville, Tenn.: American Association for State and Local History, 1970. 78 pp., illus. ◆ Provides instructions for preshipment inspection, packing, transporting and insurance. Illustrations show procedures for making photographic records and solving specific packing problems.

Keck, Caroline K.; Huntington T. Block; Joseph Chapman; John B. Lawton; and Nathan Stolow. *A Primer on Museum Security.* Cooperstown, N.Y.: New York State Historical Association, 1966. 85 pp., photos, graphs, forms, bibliog., paperback ◆ Contains basic information on physical security, insurance, environmental security, light and its effects on museum objects and other security factors.

Leene, Jentina E., ed. *Textile Conservation.* Washington, D.C.: Smithsonian Institution, 1972. 275 pp., illus., diagrams, bibliog. footnotes, index. ◆ Technical, aimed primarily at conservators. Articles on characteristics of textiles and dyestuffs, principles of cleaning and storage and techniques of restoration of flat textiles, uniforms, dresses, lace, featherwork, beadwork and leather.

National Fire Protection Association, Committee on Libraries, Museums, and Historic Buildings. *Protecting Our Heritage: A Discourse on Fire Prevention in Historic Buildings and Landmarks.* 2nd ed. Edited by Joseph F. Jenkins. Boston: National Fire Protection Association, with the assistance of the American Association for State and Local

History, 1970. 39 pp., photos, appendices, glossary of fire protection equipment, paperback. ♦ Suggests precautions which should be taken in historic buildings to prevent fires and to deal with fire emergencies if they occur. Available from National Fire Protection Association, 60 Batterymarch Street, Boston, Massachusetts 02110 or from the American Association for State and Local History, 1400 Eighth Avenue South, Nashville, Tennessee 37203.

National Research Council. Prevention of Deterioration Center. *Deterioration of Materials: Causes and Preventive Techniques.* Edited by Glenn A. Greathouse and Carl J. Wessel. New York: Reinhold Publishing Corp., 1954. 835 pp., illus., tables, charts, graphs, appendices, bibliog., index. ♦ Lists causes of destruction of every class of material, and gives preventive techniques. Very technical but the most comprehensive volume of its kind. This extremely valuable publication is, unfortunately, out-of-print. However, it is available in some libraries and is well worth consulting.

Parsons, Claudia S.M., and F.H. Curl. *China Mending and Restoration.* London: Faber and Faber, 1963. 435 pp., illus., bibliog. ♦ Discusses rivetting, dowelling, casting, overpainting and other techniques of china and glass repair. Stresses the importance of confining restoration to damaged areas and warns against excessive overpainting.

Peterson, Harold. "Conservation of Metals," *History News*, 23:2 (February 1968), Technical Leaflet no. 10. ♦ Describes basic conservation measures for iron, brass, bronze, copper, german silver, pewter, silver and gold.

Plenderleith, Harold J., and A.E.A. Werner. *The Conservation of Antiquities and Works of Art: Treatment, Repair, and Restoration.* 2nd ed. New York: Oxford University Press, 1971. 394 pp., photos, diagrams, tables, formulae, bibliog. footnotes, index. ♦ Technical, but a basic reference in the field of conservation. Includes data on the nature of the materials in museum collections, the causes of their deterioration and detailed information on methods of preservation, repair and restoration. Intended as a handbook for the collector, the archaeologist, and the museum curator, and as a workshop guide for the technician.

Sugden, Robert P. *Care and Handling of Art Objects.* New York: Metropolitan Museum of Art, 1946. 32 pp., illus., bibliog. ♦ Summary of instructions for the care and handling of art objects including paintings, large and small objects, textiles and works of art on paper. Intended to establish certain fundamental rules for the protection of objects in motion.

1

General Reference and Conservation Organizations

Represented in the first section of this chapter are abstracts, bibliographies, periodicals, and reference works, ranging from highly technical publications on special aspects of conservation to general volumes on preventive care and maintenance and first aid measures to meet the ravages of fire or flood. The difference in approach is illustrated by the volumes written by Plenderleith and Guldbeck: the former is for the professional conservator, while the latter was written, at the request of the American Association for State and Local History, for the nonspecialist.

The second section of this chapter describes the major organizations and agencies concerned with the conservation of historic and artistic resources. They comprise the leadership in a small but dedicated profession which has done much to raise public consciousness about the care and conservation of collections. There is a description of the purposes, scope, professional services and publications of each organization. They should be supported generously and widely, for they are the medium for establishing and maintaining standards in a field where commercialism rather than professionalism is sometimes triumphant.

There are many other organizations and agencies that are committed to the goals of conservation but are not described here. They include the American Association for State and Local History, the American Association of Museums, the International Council of Museums, the National Endowment for the Arts, the Smithsonian Institution (National Museum Act), and some major museums and historical societies. Also, many states are instituting programs for conservation care that try to reach out beyond state-owned collections.

General Reference

"Abstracts of the Rome Conference Contributions, September 1961," *Studies in Conservation,* 6:4 (November 1961), entire issue. ◆ Includes lighting, humidity control, packing, transport, methods of analysis, fungicides and insecticides, cleaning of paintings, treatment of metallic objects, consolidation of fragile objects, examination and conservation of glass, reinforcing and transfer of wood panel paintings, new picture varnishes, treatment and repair of textiles and tapestries, education and training of conservators and restorers.

Agrawal, O.P., ed. *Conservation of Cultural Property in India. Proceedings of the II Seminar, February 8, 1967.* New Delhi: Indian Association for the Study of Conservation, 1967. 94 pp.

Agrawal, O.P., ed. *Conservation of Cultural Property in India. Proceedings of the III Seminar, May 24-25, 1969.* New Delhi: Indian

4

Association for the Study of Conservation, 1969. 41 pp.

American Association of Museums. *The Condition and Needs of America's Museums. A Report to the Federal Council on the Arts and Humanities by a Special Committee of the American Association of Museums.* Washington, D.C.: The Association, 1968. 96 pp. ◆ Includes an evaluation of the problem of conservation and what must be done about it.

Barker, Harold. "Scientific Criteria in the Authentication of Antiquities." In *Application of Science in the Examination of Works of Art: Proceedings of the Seminar: June 15–19, 1970* (Boston: Museum of Fine Arts, 1973), pp. 187–192. ◆ Examination techniques, dating methods, studies in technology.

Blomquist, Richard F. *Adhesives—Past, Present and Future.* Philadelphia, Pa.: American Society for Testing and Materials, 1964. 34 pp., illus., bibliog.

Boston. Museum of Fine Arts. Research Laboratory. *Application of Science in the Examination of Works of Art; Proceedings of the Seminar: September 15–18, 1958.* Boston: The Museum, 1959. 198 pp., illus., diagrams, tables, bibliog. ◆ A collection of papers presented at the seminar. Specific articles have been listed by author in the appropriate chapters.

Boston. Museum of Fine Arts. Research Laboratory. *Application of Science in the Examination of Works of Art; Proceedings of the Seminar: September 7–16, 1965.* Boston: The Museum, 1967. 254 pp., illus., maps, bibliog. ◆ A collection of papers presented at the seminar. Specific articles have been listed by author in the appropriate chapters.

Boston. Museum of Fine Arts. Research Laboratory. *Application of Science in the Examination of Works of Art; Proceedings of the Seminar: June 15–19, 1970.* Boston: The Museum, 1973. 271 pp., illus., maps, charts. ◆ A collection of papers presented at the seminar. Specific articles have been listed by author in the appropriate chapters.

Braude, Felix. *Adhesives.* Brooklyn, N.Y.: Chemical Publishing Co., 1943. 154 pp., tables, bibliog. footnotes.

Brill, T.B., and G.J. Reilly. "Chemistry in the Museum," *Chemistry,* 45:5 (May 1972), pp. 6–9.

Buck, Richard. "On Conservation: Inspection of Collections," *Museum News,* 52:3 (November 1973), pp. 12–13.

Buck, Richard. "On Conservation: Regional Conservation Centers," *Museum News,* 52:8 (May 1974), pp. 10-11.

Buck, Richard. "On Conservation: The Future," *Museum News,* 52:9 (June 1974), pp. 21-22.

Buck, Richard. "On Conservation: The Report on a Laboratory Examination," *Museum News,* 52:4 (December 1973), pp. 15-16.

Buck, Richard. "On Conservation: What is Conservation," *Museum News,* 52:1 (September 1973), pp. 15-16. ◆ Makes distinctions between restoration, preservation, and conservation.

Buck, Richard D. "On the Conservation of Works of Art," *Art Association of Indianapolis Bulletin,* 54 (March 1967), pp. 5-26.

Cagle, Charles V. *Adhesive Bonding: Technique and Application.* New York: McGraw-Hill Book Co., 1968. 351 pp., illus., bibliog.

"Canadians Glimpse New Techniques in Travelling Conservation Exhibit," *History News,* 28:4 (April 1973), pp. 74-75.

Colonial Williamsburg, Film Distribution Section. *The Art of the Conservator.* With Russell J. Quandt and Robert Feller. Film, 57 minutes, 16 mm., color, sound (1966); and, 28½ minutes, 16 mm., color, sound (1972). ◆ Explains methods and reasoning used by conservators. Shows investigative techniques, relining, cleaning, filling, and inpainting.

The Conservation of Cultural Property, with Special Reference to Tropical Conditions. Museums and Monuments, XI. Paris: UNESCO, 1968. 341 pp., photos, drawings, diagrams, tables, maps, formulae, appendices, bibliog., index. ◆ Articles by experts in the field on climate and microclimate, moulds, insects, conservation of glass, stone, metals, textiles, leather, wood, archival materials and paintings; recommendations on lighting, air conditioning, storage and handling. Very technical but an excellent reference on the problems of conservation in the tropics.

Constable, William G. "Curatorial Problems in Relation to Conservation," *Museum News,* 24:9 (November 1, 1946), pp. 6-8.

Daifuku, Hiroshi. "The Significance of Cultural Property." In *The Conservation of Cultural Property with Special Reference to Tropical Conditions* (Paris: UNESCO, 1968), pp. 19-26. ◆ Includes definition, problem of choice, legislation, conservation and the public, bilateral and international programs, conservation and restoration, keeping records, and bibliography.

Delmonte, John. *The Technology of Adhesives.* 1947. Reprint. New York: Hafner Publishing Co., 1965. 516 pp., illus., bibliog. ◆ Facsimile of the 1947 edition.

Dudley, Dorothy H., and Irma B. Wilkinson, et al. *Museum Registration Methods.* Rev. ed. Washington, D.C.: American Association of Museums, 1968. 294 pp., illus., forms, plans, bibliog., index. ◆ Covers aspects of storage, packing, registration, classification and inspection of art objects and includes a trial glossary for describing condition. Revised edition in progress.

Gettens, Rutherford J., and George L. Stout. *Painting Materials: A Short Encyclopedia.* 1942. Reprint. New York: Dover Publications, 1966. 333 pp., illus., bibliog., glossary, paperback. ◆ A reliable source of information on materials used as supports, grounds, pigments, media, adhesives, varnishes and solvents and on equipment and tools, in painting past and present. A valuable reference for professional conservators and research scholars.

Gettens, Rutherford J., and Bertha M. Usilton, comps. *Abstracts of Technical Studies in Art and Archaeology, 1943–1952.* Smithsonian Institution, Freer Gallery of Art, Occasional Papers, 2:2, Publication 4176. Washington, D.C.: Smithsonian Institution, 1955. 408 pp., index.

Gilbert, Edward R. "Curatorial Responsibilities and Conservation." AASLH Cassette Tape no. 6. Nashville, Tenn.: American Association for State and Local History, 1971. 1 cassette tape, 59 minutes. ◆ An examination of the harmful effects of sunlight, air, insects, pests, micro-organisms, and neglect, including what can be done to preserve artifacts exposed to these hazards and materials to be used. Also a discussion of restoration and preservation with emphasis on attitudes, precautions, reversible processes, and accurate records.

Gorine, Ivan. "The Restoration of Works of Art in the U.S.S.R.," *Museum,* XX:2 (1967), pp. 116-123.

Guldbeck, Per E. *The Care of Historical Collections: A Conservation Handbook for the Non-Specialist.* Rev. ed. Nashville, Tenn.: American Association for State and Local History, 1972. 160 pp., photos, drawings, diagrams, tables, bibliog., supply list, appendices, paperback. ◆ Provides an introduction to the problems of conservation and describes basic procedures for the care of museum collections. Includes advice on the treatment of paper, wood, leather, textiles, ceramics and related materials. Deals with the environmental aspects of conservation, documentation of artifacts, and the equipment of a conservation laboratory. Intended as a practical manual for the small historical society or museum.

Guldbeck, Per E. "Conservation and Care of Collections." AASLH Cassette Tape no. 16. Nashville, Tenn.: American Association for State and Local History, 1971. 1 cassette tape, 57 minutes. ◆ Explains what conservation is in respect to restoration and reviews details of techniques and materials used in fire protection, cleaning and repairing items, keeping records, cautions in the cleaning process, collection care and storage, and security for the collection.

Hamblin, Dora Jane. "Science Finds Way to Restore the Art Damage in Florence," *Smithsonian,* 4:11 (February 1974), pp. 26-35.

Harvard University, William Hayes Fogg Art Museum. *Technical Studies in the Field of the Fine Arts.* Cambridge, Mass.: Harvard University Press, 1932-42. 10 vols. ◆ An invaluable source of information on materials, techniques, environmental control, technical examination and conservation and restoration procedures. This pioneer work has been reprinted in photo-facsimile with a cumulative index. Available from: Garland Publishing, Inc., 10 East 44th Street, New York, New York 10017. It is very expensive however, and should probably be considered for purchase by libraries rather than individuals.

Hedvall, J. Arvid. "Objects of Cultural Value and Knowledge of Materials," *Museum,* V:1 1952), pp. 39-52.

Held, Julius. *Alteration and Mutilation of Works of Art.* Raleigh, N.C.: Duke University Press, 1963. 28 pp., illus. ◆ Reprinted from *South Atlantic Quarterly,* LXII:1 (Winter 1963), pp. 1–27. Describes historical changes, intentional and otherwise, inflicted on works of art with critical evaluations of their causes.

Horton, Carolyn. *Cleaning and Preserving Bindings and Related Materials.* 2nd ed., rev. Chicago: Library Technology Project, American Library Association, 1969. 87 pp., illus., bibliog., paperback. ◆ Includes information on reconditioning a library, sorting books and identifying problems and treatment of worn and damaged books; list of supplies and equipment, sources of supply and a glossary. This helpful and clearly written book provides much practical advice to the novice.

International Biodeterioration Symposium, 1st, Southampton, Eng., 1968. *Biodeterioration of Materials; Microbiological and Allied Aspects.* Edited by Harry Walters and John J. Elphiet. Amsterdam, N.Y.: Elsevier Publishing Co., 1969. 740 pp., illus., bibliog. ◆ Available in English or French.

International Biodeterioration Symposium, 2nd, Lunteren, Netherlands, 1971. *Biodeterioration of Materials. Proceedings.* New York: Wiley (Halsted Press Div.), 1972. 514 pp., illus., diagrams. ◆ Presents a wide range of up-to-date information on the effects of biodeterioration due to both macro and microbiological causes. One section is devoted to the effects of biodeterioration on objects of art and science. Problems discussed include preservation of remains of ancient buildings; choice of suitable biocides for the treatment and protection of library and archival material; the action of biological agents on works of art in Venice; fungal testing of textiles.

International Centre for the Study of the Preservation and the Restoration of Cultural Property. "Synthetic Materials Used in the Conservation of Cultural Property." In *The Conservation of Cultural Property with Special Reference to Tropical Conditions* (Paris: UNESCO, 1968), pp. 303–335. ◆ Discusses thermoplastic varnishes, transparent sheets, adhesives and consolidants. Includes an index of trade names and an index of producers.

International Centre for the Study of the Preservation and the Restoration of Cultural Property. *Synthetic Materials Used in the Conservation of Cultural Property.* Rome: The Centre, 1963. 67 pp., bibliog., tables. ◆ Discusses thermoplastic varnishes, laminants, adhesives and consolidants, and ultraviolet absorbers. Revised and updated in *The Conservation of Cultural Property with Special Reference to Tropical Conditions.* See previous reference.

Intergovernmental Conference on the Protection of Cultural Property in the Event of Armed Conflict. *Records of the Conference Convened by the United Nations Educational, Scientific and Cultural Organization Held at The Hague from 21 April to 14 May, 1954.* The Hague: Government of the Netherlands, 1961. 452 pp.

Intergovernmental Conference on the Protection of Cultural Property in the Event of Armed Conflict, The Hague, 1954. *Final Act, Convention and Protocol Adopted by the United Nations Conference on the Protection of Cultural Property in the Event of Armed Conflict, Together with Regulations for the Execution of the Convention and Resolutions Attached to the Final Act, The Hague, May 14, 1954.* London: Her Majesty's Stationery Office, 1954. 49 pp.

International Institute for Conservation of Historic and Artistic Works. *Recent Advances in Conservation, Contributions to the IIC Rome Conference, 1961.* Edited by G. Thomson. London: Butterworths, 1963. 224 pp., illus., bibliog. ◆ Discusses museum climate; physical and chemical methods of analysis; fungicides and insecticides; application of science to cleaning; examination and treatment of metallic objects; Italian methods of fresco transfer; consolidation of fragile objects; examination and conservation of glass; transfer of wood panel paintings; treatment of textiles and tapestries; education and training of conservators. Specific articles have been listed by author in the appropriate chapters.

International Institute for Conservation of Historic and Artistic Works—American Group. *IIC—American Group Technical Papers from 1968 Through 1970.* New York: IIC—American Group, 1970. 179 pp., illus. ◆ Specific articles have been listed by author in the appropriate chapters.

Keck, Caroline K. "Conservation: Where Conservation Begins," *History News,* 29:2 (February 1974), p. 32. ♦ Discusses curatorial maintenance of collections.

Keck, Caroline K. "Conservators, Collections and Acquisition," *Museum News,* 50:1 (September 1971), pp. 39–42. ♦ Functions of a conservator: examination, treatment, maintenance.

Keck, Caroline K. "On Conservation: Caring for Your Collections," *Museum News,* 50:3 (November 1971), p. 9. ♦ How to find and prepare for a conservator.

Keck, Caroline K. "On Conservation: Locating Competent Practitioners," *Museum News,* 50:6 (February 1972), p. 9. ♦ How to recognize competent practitioners.

Keck, Caroline K. "Technical Assistance: Where to Find It, What to Expect," *Curator,* VIII:3 (1965), pp. 197–211.

Keck, Caroline K.; Huntington T. Block; Joseph Chapman; John B. Lawton; and Nathan Stolow. *A Primer on Museum Security.* Cooperstown, N.Y.: New York State Historical Association, 1966. 85 pp., photos, graphs, forms, bibliog., paperback. ♦ Contains basic information on physical security, insurance, environmental security, light and its effects on museum objects and other security factors.

Keisch, Bernard. "Art and the Atom: Two Dating Methods Based on Measurements of Radioactivity." In *Application of Science in the Examination of Works of Art; Proceedings of the Seminar: June 15–19, 1970* (Boston: Museum of Fine Arts, 1970), pp. 193–198.

Keisch, Bernard. *Secrets of the Past: Nuclear Energy Applications in Art and Archaeology.* Washington, D.C.: U.S. Atomic Energy Commission, Office of Information Services, 1972. 119 pp., photos, charts, bibliog., paperback. ♦ Nuclear techniques in archeology: dating, fingerprinting, general analysis. Nuclear techniques in art: dating, fingerprinting, general analysis, restoration of old photographs, conservation of wood and other porous materials.

Kinard, Epsie. *The Care and Keeping of Antiques.* New York: Hawthorne Press, 1972. 160 pp., illus., bibliog., paperback. ♦ Contents include oil paintings, pastels, prints, brass, bronze, copper, crystal, clocks, frames, furniture, ivory and bone, iron, lead, marble and slate, music boxes, pewter, porcelain and earthenware, silver, textiles, tinware, wall hangings, wooden flooring, woodenware.

Leavitt, Thomas W. "Conservation in a Small Museum," *Museum News,* 49:7 (March 1971), pp. 22–24. ♦ Merrimack Valley Textile Museum exhibit, "Techniques of Print Conservation and Analysis."

Levenson, Rustin. "Conservation Queries," *Canadian Conservation Institute Newsletter,* November 1973–.

McEwing, Roy. "Seasons of the Mind: Mind Preserved," *UNESCO Courier,* 24:8 (August–September 1971), pp. 48–53. ♦ UNESCO's efforts to preserve monuments of the past.

Majewski, Lawrence J. "Every Museum Library Should Have . . . ," *Museum News,* 52:3 (November 1973), pp. 27–30. ♦ A bibliography of books on conservation for the small museum library.

Majewski, Lawrence J. "On Conservation: Conservation Research," *Museum News,* 51:9 (May 1973), pp. 18–19.

Mates, Robert E. *Photographing Art.* Philadelphia: Chilton Books, 1966. 128 pp., illus., bibliog. ♦ Techniques used by a museum staff photographer to photograph paintings, drawings, watercolors, collages, sculpture, and a variety of art objects.

Miner, Ralph W., Jr. *Conservation of Historic and Cultural Resources.* Chicago: American Society of Planning Officials, 1969. 56 pp., photos, bibliog., paperback. ♦ Defines historic and cultural conservation; traces the changing emphases of the preservation movement; and outlines an approach to a comprehensive program through surveys, legal techniques, public and private options.

Moss, A.A. *Application of X-Rays, Gamma Rays, Ultra-Violet and Infra-Red Rays to the Study of Antiquities.* Handbook for Museum Curators, Part B, Section 4, Museum Technique. London: The Museums Association, 1954. 16 pp., illus., bibliog. ♦ Introduction to the theory and practice of special radiations in the study of works of art and antiquities.

National Association of Mutual Casualty Companies. *Handbook of Organic Industrial*

Solvents. Chicago: The Association, 1958. 71 pp.

National Research Council. Prevention of Deterioration Center. *Deterioration of Materials: Causes and Preventive Techniques.* Edited by Glenn A. Greathouse and Carl J. Wessel. New York: Reinhold Publishing Corp., 1954. 835 pp., illus., tables, charts, graphs, appendices, bibliog., index. ◆ Lists causes of destruction of every class of material, and gives preventive techniques. This extremely valuable publication is, unfortunately, out-of-print. However, it is available in some libraries and is well worth consulting.

Noblecourt, André. *Protection of Cultural Property in the Event of Armed Conflict.* Museums and Monuments, VIII. Paris: UNESCO, 1958. 346 pp., illus., bibliog.

Ogilvie, Robert E. "Applications of the Solid State X-Ray Detector to the Study of Art Objects." In *Application of Science in the Examination of Works of Art; Proceedings of the Seminar: June 15–19, 1970* (Boston: Museum of Fine Arts, 1973), pp. 84–87. ◆ Electron microanalysis and x-ray excitation.

Ormsbee, Thomas H. *Care and Repair of Antiques.* New York: Medill, McBride Co., 1949. 168 pp., illus.

Payne, Henry Fleming. *Organic Coating Technology.* New York: Wiley & Sons, 1954–61. 2 vols.

Plenderleith, Harold J. "The New Science of Art Conservation," *UNESCO Courier,* 18 (January 1965), pp. 7–10.

Plenderleith, Harold J., and A.E.A. Werner. *The Conservation of Antiquities and Works of Art: Treatment, Repair and Restoration.* 2nd ed. New York: Oxford University Press, 1971. 394 pp., photos, diagrams, tables, formulae, bibliog. footnotes, index. ◆ Technical but a basic reference in the field of conservation. Includes data on the nature of the materials in museum collections; the causes of their deterioration; and detailed information on methods of preservation, repair and restoration. Intended as a handbook for the collector, the archeologist, and the museum curator, and as a workshop guide for the technician.

Problems of Conservation in Museums. A Selection of Papers Presented to the Joint Meeting of the ICOM Committee for Museum Laboratories and the ICOM Committee for the Care of Paintings. Paris: Editions Eyrolles, 1969. 223 pp., illus., graphs, photos, diagrams, bibliog. references, glossary, appendices. ◆ Includes chapters on training of restorers, deterioration and treatment of wood, deterioration of cellulose, lamination of documents.

Ratcliff, Rosemary. *Refurbishing Antiques.* Chicago: Regnery, 1971. 209 pp., illus. ◆ Includes chapters on furniture, paintings, prints, books, metal, silver, china, glass, clocks, dolls, etc.

Riley, Orrin H., and Gustav A. Berger. "New Developments in the Conservation of Works of Art," *Art Journal,* 31:1 (Fall 1971), pp. 37–40.

Sekino, Masaru, and Kenzo Toishi. "The Fine Arts Museum at Expo '70, Osaka: Conservation Techniques," *Museum,* XXIV:1 (1972), pp. 67–88. ◆ Discusses security, air conditioning, heating, lighting, temperature and humidity, monitoring systems.

Skeist, Irving, ed. *Handbook of Adhesives.* New York: Reinhold Publishing Co., 1962. 683 pp., illus.

Spencer, John. "Conservation's Paradoxical Crisis," *Art in America,* 61:4 (July–August 1973), p. 11.

Stolow, Nathan. "Gas Chromatography and Pyrolysis Techniques to Establish Ageing Characteristics of Works of Art." In *Application of Science in the Examination of Works of Art; Proceedings of the Seminar: June 15–19, 1970* (Boston: Museum of Fine Arts, 1973), pp. 213–228.

Sugden, Robert P. *Care and Handling of Art Objects.* New York: Metropolitan Museum of Art, 1946. 32 pp., illus., bibliog. ◆ Summary of instructions for the care and handling of art objects including paintings, large and small objects, textiles and works of art on paper. Intended to establish certain fundamental rules for the protection of objects in motion.

"They Work Against Time: Art's Silent Partners," *The Laboratory,* 29:3 (1961), pp. 66–70. ◆ Describes the work of the conservators at the National Gallery of Canada.

Thomson, Garry. "The Conservation of Antiquities: Developments in Planning," *Journal of World History,* XIV:1 (1972), pp. 24–47.

Thomson, Garry. "Impermanence—Some Chemical and Physical Aspects," *Museums Journal,* 64:1 (June 1964), pp. 16–36.

Thomson, Garry. "Planning the Preservation of Our Cultural Heritage," *Museum,* XXV:1–2 (1973), pp. 15–25.

United Nations Educational, Scientific and Cultural Organization. *The Organization of Museums; Practical Advice.* Museums and Monuments, IX. Paris: UNESCO, 1960. 188 pp., illus., bibliog.

U.S. National Park Service. *Field Manual for Museums.* 1941. Reprint. Ann Arbor, Mich.: Finch Press, 1974. 426 pp., illus., plans, bibliog. ◆ Originally published by the U.S. Government Printing Office.

U.S. National Park Service. "Technical Methods." In *Field Manual for Museums* (Ann Arbor, Mich.: Finch Press, 1974), pp. 118–239.

Yamasaki, Kazuo. "Recent Technical Studies of Works of Art in Japan." In *Application of Science in the Examination of Works of Art; Proceedings of the Seminar: June 15–19, 1970* (Boston: Museum of Fine Arts, 1973), pp. 229–234.

Young, W.J. "Examination of Works of Art Embracing the Various Fields of Science." In *Application of Science in the Examination of Works of Art; Proceedings of the Seminar: September 15–18, 1958* (Boston: Museum of Fine Arts, 1959), pp. 17–30.

NOTES AND PERIODICALS

Art and Archaeology Technical Abstracts. 1955, irreg. (approx. 2/yr.), subscription. Circulation Dept., AATA, c/o New York University, Conservation Center, Institute of Fine Arts, 1 East 78th Street, New York, New York 10021. ◆ Analytical bibliography of the world literature relating to conservation technology. Also includes annotated bibliographies on special subjects. Formerly *IIC Abstracts.*

Bulletin of the American Institute for Conservation of Historic and Artistic Works. 1960, two issues per year, membership. Subscriptions to Mrs. Barbara H. Beardsley, Director of Bulletin Subscriptions, Dudley Homestead, Raymond, New Hampshire 03077. ◆ Many useful articles on topics relating to conservation and restoration. Formerly called *Bulletin of the American Group–IIC;* new title as of vol. 13, no. 2 (1973).

Canadian Conservation Institute Newsletter. 1973, quarterly, membership. Canadian Conservation Institute, National Museums of Canada, Ottawa, Ontario, Canada K1A OM8.

Conservation Information Program, c/o Elena Borosky, Office of Museum Programs, Smithsonian Institution, Washington, D.C. 20560. ◆ A series of slide presentations on conservation are being produced by the Smithsonian Institution. The audiovisual units, aimed at historical societies and small museums, include information on a variety of current conservation practices. Each may be borrowed for two weeks at no charge except return postage.

ICA Newsletter. 1952, two issues per year, membership. Intermuseum Conservation Association, Allen Art Building, Oberlin, Ohio 44074. ◆ Contains valuable technical and background information not available elsewhere.

ICOM News. 1948, quarterly, membership or subscription. International Council of Museums, 6 Rue Miollis, Paris XVe, France.

IIC News. Supplement to *Studies in Conservation.* 1960, two issues per year, membership. International Institute for Conservation of Historic and Artistic Works, 608 Grand Buildings, Trafalgar Square, London WC 2N 5HN, England. ◆ General news of institute activities and occasional technical information. Ceased separate publication with vol. 5, 1969. It is now combined with *Studies in Conservation.*

Studies in Conservation/Etudes de Conservation. 1952, quarterly, membership or subscription. International Institute for Conservation of Historic and Artistic Works, 608 Grand Buildings, Trafalgar Square, London WC 2N 5HN, England. ◆ A quarterly journal carrying original scientific and practical papers on new methods applied to and problems involved in the conservation and restoration of objects.

Technology and Conservation. 1976, quarterly, free to qualified persons, subscription to nonqualified persons. The Technology Organization, Inc., 1 Emerson Place, Boston, Massachusetts 02114.

Conservation Organizations

American Institute for Conservation of Historic and Artistic Works, Inc. (AIC), c/o C T Corporation System, 918 16th Street, N.W., Washington, D.C. 20006.

The American Institute for Conservation of Historic and Artistic Works, formerly American Group—IIC, became in 1973, an independent incorporated professional organization in order to obtain tax exempt status and the right to receive tax deductible contributions. It still, however, retains its affiliation with IIC. The AIC was formed to provide an organization for persons engaged in the preservation and restoration of historic and artistic works in order that they may exchange, coordinate and advance knowledge and improved methods of art conservation.

PUBLICATIONS: *Bulletin of the American Institute for Conservation of Historic and Artistic Works,* published twice yearly, reports on activities, personal news, technical notes, annual meeting papers and reports.

Canadian Conservation Institute (CCI), National Museums of Canada, Ottawa, K1A 0M8, Canada.

The Canadian Conservation Institute was established in 1972 by the National Museums of Canada as a branch of the federal museum system. The organization of the Institute is national in scope, consisting of a headquarters in Ottawa, and five regional centers across Canada (Atlantic, Pacific, Prairies, Ontario, Quebec).

PROFESSIONAL SERVICES: provides conservation services to Canadian museums and carries out relevant research in conservation.

PUBLICATIONS: *Canadian Conservation Institute Newsletter,* a quarterly publication containing news of the activities of the Institute, technical notes, and a "Conservation Queries" column.

Intermuseum Conservation Association (ICA), Allen Art Building, Oberlin, Ohio 44074.

The Intermuseum Conservation Association was established in 1952 as a cooperative association of midwestern museums. Membership includes sixteen museums, and through the Intermuseum Laboratory, conservation services are provided to these museums on a nonprofit basis. Each museum makes a yearly contribution to the Association based on a scale related to the individual museum's annual budget. Work on objects is billed to the owner museum, based on a schedule of hourly rates. One representative from each museum serves on the Board of Trustees which establishes laboratory policy.

PROFESSIONAL SERVICES: Makes a yearly inspection trip to each member museum to examine collections and make minor repairs; provides treatment of works of art, primarily paintings.

PUBLICATIONS: *ICA Newsletter,* published twice yearly, provides news of the Association's activities, laboratory notes, and short articles on aspects of conservation;

Curatorial Care of Works of Art on Paper by Anne F. Clapp; *On Picture Varnishes and Their Solvents* by Feller, Stolow and Jones.

International Centre for the Study of the Preservation and the Restoration of Cultural Property (Rome Centre), 13 Via di San Michele, 00153, Rome, Italy. In the U.S., contact United States International Centre Committee, Advisory Council for Historic Preservation, 1522 K Street, Suite 430, Washington, D.C. 20005.

The International Centre was created by UNESCO in 1958 "to build the strongest bastion possible against the forces of destruction." Its purposes are to collect, study and circulate documentation concerned with the scientific and technical problems of the preservation and restoration of cultural property; to coordinate, encourage, or carry out research by means of commissions, international meetings, publications and exchanges of specialists; to give advice and recommendations on problems concerned with the preservation and restoration of cultural property; to assist in training researchers and technicians and in raising the standards of restoration work.

MEMBERSHIP: The International Centre is an inter-governmental autonomous, scientific institution, the membership of which comprises fifty-eight member countries throughout the world. Each member pays an amount equal to 1% of its annual contribution to UNESCO. Associate membership is available to public or private non-profit institutions by paying a subscription fixed by the Centre's Council.

ORGANIZATION: The Constitution of the Centre provides for a General Assembly consisting of representatives of member countries and meeting once every two years to determine and approve program and budget; a Council of Specialists, most of whom are selected by the General Assembly; a Secretariat responsible for the preparation and execution of the Centre's program.

PROFESSIONAL SERVICES: Maintains, for the use of specialists and students, a library and documentation service in all fields of conservation of cultural property; conducts three training courses annually: Architectural Conservation, Fundamental Principles of Conservation, and Conservation of Mural Paintings (descriptions of these courses may be found in the chapter on Training of Conservators); organizes individual study courses in various specialized national institutions; offers specialized assistance to members of the Centre including technical correspondence, expert missions, organization of pilot work sites, rescue missions in times of catastrophe.

OTHER SERVICES: Organizes meetings of specialists, in cooperation with ICOM, ICOMOS, and IIC; delegates specific tasks to experts in the form of research contracts; organizes regional seminars to aid the development of conservation in various parts of the world.

PUBLICATIONS: *Works and Publications*, basic works in their original language or translated, and published jointly with ICOM Committee for Conservation; *Technical Notes,* a series designed for students attending courses organized by the Centre.

International Council of Museums (ICOM), Committee for Conservation, Maison de l'UNESCO, 1 Rue Miollis, Paris XVe, France.

The ICOM Conservation Committee was organized in 1967 to offer to specialists concerned with conservation (curators, art historians, archeologists, restorers) a framework within which to cooperate on a interdisciplinary and international level. The Committee is composed of a Directory Board and a series of working groups, each concerned with a particular area of conservation. The Directory Board is elected by members of the working groups.

ACTIVITIES: Triennial plenary meetings are held at which progress reports are presented by the working groups. These reports constitute either a critical bibliography on a given subject, or reports on research. These texts, considered as unpublished works, are reproduced by the Documentation Service of the International Centre for the Study of the Preservation and the Restoration of Cultural Property and are available at cost price.

International Institute for Conservation of Historic and Artistic Works (IIC), 608 Grand Buildings, Trafalgar Square, London WC 2N 5HN, England.

The International Institute for Conservation of Historic and Artistic Works was founded in 1950 to provide a permanent, international organization to coordinate and improve the knowledge, methods and working standards needed to protect and preserve materials of cultural value. Its primary function is to supply information or research into all processes connected with conservation, both scientific and technical, and on the development of those processes.

MEMBERSHIP: There are four categories of membership in the IIC. Honorary Fellowship is conferred by the Council of IIC upon persons who have rendered outstanding service to the field of conservation. Fellowship is a professional qualification open to specialists of outstanding ability directly concerned with conservation. Election to fellowship is normally from the Associate grade. Associateship is open to anyone who is interested in the aims of the Institute. Institutional membership is open to any corporate body interested in the aims of the Institute.

ACTIVITIES: International Congresses are held every two or three years in appropriate centers. Papers commissioned from leading specialists are read and discussed. The aims of the congresses are to summarize the present position of technical progress in the particular field and to present recent advances and research. Regional Groups, with the approval of the Council, operate autonomously in several countries. These groups form centers for the exchange of professional information among members and hold periodic meetings whose proceedings are circulated.

PUBLICATIONS: *Studies in Conservation*, a quarterly journal carrying original scientific and practical papers on new methods applied to and problems involved in the conservation and restoration of objects; *IIC News* provides news of conferences and seminars, activities of members and notes and articles on recent work and new materials and is distributed with *Studies in Conservation; Art and Archaeology Technical Abstracts,* a twice yearly analytical bibliography of the world's literature relating to conservation technology and also carries supplements which are extensive, annotated bibliographies on special subjects.

13

The IIC also publishes books on aspects of conservation in conjunction with international congresses and sponsors books on specialized subjects within its field. These include *Textile Conservation*—IIC Delft Conference, 1964; *Museum Climatology*—IIC London Conference, 1967; *Conservation of Stone and Wooden Objects*—IIC New York Conference, 1970; *Conservation of Paintings and the Graphic Arts*—IIC Lisbon Conference, 1972.

National Conservation Advisory Council c/o Office of Museum Programs, Smithsonian Institution, Washington, D.C. 20560.

The National Conservation Advisory Council was formed in 1974 to foster planning and cooperation between conservation institutions and programs in the United States; to seek ways to meet needs in training and research; to explore the possibility of using data processing techniques for this material. Membership on the Council includes, but is not limited to, members of the International Centre and the Advisory Council on Historic Preservation.

ACTIVITIES: The Council will study the feasibility of creating a national conservation institute and will prepare an annual report to be distributed to the International Centre Committee, American Association of Museums, and other interested groups. Committees organized to carry out these activities include education and training, a study committee, research and publication, and membership.

2

Philosophy, History, and Principles of Conservation

For many years professional conservators have been waging a quiet, intensive battle to assure the integrity of the artifacts being conserved and to establish standards of practice. Their achievements have provided historical agency personnel with convincing arguments for the value and necessity of conservation. The information provided by the references in this chapter can be used to good advantage in persuading trustees of the urgent need to implement a conservation program of remedial treatment and preventive maintenance to insure the survival of the collections for which they are responsible.

Brommelle, Norman. "Materials for a History of Conservation," *Studies in Conservation*, 2:4 (October 1956), pp. 176–186.

Buck, Richard. "On Conservation: What is Condition," *Museum News*, 52:2 (October 1973), pp. 15–16.

Buck, Richard D. "What is Condition in a Work of Art," *Bulletin of the American Group—IIC*, 12:1 (October 1971), pp. 63–67.

Constable, William G. "Curatorial Problems in Relation to Conservation," *Museum News*, 24:9 (November 1, 1946), pp. 6–8.

Gregg, Richard N. "The Modest Museum and Its Borrowing Needs," *Bulletin of the American Group—IIC*, 11:1 (October 1970), pp. 5–8.

Held, Julius. *Alteration and Mutilation of Works of Art.* Raleigh, N.C.: Duke University Press, 1963. 28 pp., illus. ◆ Reprinted from *South Atlantic Quarterly*, LXII:1 (Winter 1963), pp. 1–27. Describes historical changes, intentional and otherwise, inflicted on works of art with critical evaluations of their causes.

IIC-AG Committee on Professional Standards and Procedures. *The Murray Pease Report and Code of Ethics for Art Conservators.*

New York: The Committee, 1968. 68 pp., paperback. ◆ Serves as a guide for consumer protection; provides guidelines for evaluating a conservator's service.

International Museum Office. *Manual on the Conservation of Paintings.* Paris: The Office, 1940. 296 pp., illus., paperback.

Keck, Caroline K. "History and Philosophy of Conservation," *Bulletin of the American Group—IIC*, 5:1 (October 1964), pp. 1–3.

Keck, Sheldon. "A Little Training Can Be a Dangerous Thing," *Museum News*, 52:4 (December 1973), pp. 40–42. ◆ Advocates an extended course in curatorial conservation responsibilities in regular museum training programs.

London. National Gallery. *An Exhibition of Cleaned Pictures (1936–1947).* London: Printed for the Trustees, 1947. 104 pp., glossary, bibliog. ◆ Foreword by Philip Hendy presents arguments in favor of painting conservation.

Miner, Ralph W., Jr. *Conservation of Historic and Cultural Resources.* Chicago: American Society of Planning Officials, 1969. 56 pp., illus., photos, bibliog., paperback. ◆ Defines historic and cultural conservation; traces the changing emphases of the preservation movement; and outlines an approach to a comprehensive program through surveys, legal techniques, public and private options.

Noble, Joseph V. "Museum Manifesto," *Museum News,* 48:8 (April 1970), pp. 16–20. ♦ Discusses the five basic areas of responsibility for museums: acquisitions, conservation, study, interpretation and exhibition.

Pease, Murray, et al. "The Pease Report," *Studies in Conservation,* 9:3 (August 1964), pp. 116–121.

Pomerantz, Louis. "Know What You See," *Museum News,* 50:4 (December 1971), pp. 16–23.

Stout, George L. "Treatment of Blemished Paintings," *Technical Studies in the Field of the Fine Arts,* X:2 (October 1941), pp. 99–112.

3

Conservation Laboratories and Instrumentation

Nowhere is the science of conservation of works of art more apparent than in a well-designed, well-equipped conservation laboratory. Machinery and equipment used in analysis and treatment includes ultraviolet and infrared lights; instruments for electron probe microanalysis and optical emission spectrometry; balances; hot tables; special cameras and darkrooms. Equally important are the files of the written and photographic documentation of the conservation process.

In truth, there are not many such laboratories in the United States today. Largely, this is because the physical, mechanical and technical requirements of conservation are substantial and because there is a serious dearth of competent, trained practitioners. Conservation is a human endeavor combining dedication of head, heart, and hands with the finest instrumentation. For those interested in supplying fine working conditions and equipment, references on laboratory design and on the necessary furnishings, tools, instruments and supplies are cited below.

Al-Naqshbandi, Ali. "The Iraq Museum Laboratory, Baghdad," *Studies in Conservation,* 18:1 (February 1973), pp. 36–42.

Block, Huntington T. "Insurance in the Conservation Laboratory, Part I," *Bulletin of the American Group—IIC,* 1:2 (April 1961), pp. 5–7. ◆ A basic understanding of procedures as they relate to conservation matters.

Brommelle, N.S. "Laboratories and Workshops—Conservation Studios," *Museums Journal,* 63:1–2 (June–September 1963), pp. 74–79.

"A Conservation Workroom," *Intermuseum Conservation Association Newsletter,* 4:2 (October 1966), pp. 2–5. ◆ A listing of the conditions, furnishings, tools and supplies needed for setting up an arts conservation workshop.

Coremans, Paul. "The Museum Laboratory." In *Organization of Museums: Practical Advice* (Paris: UNESCO, 1969), pp. 93–118. ◆ A general survey of the functions of a museum laboratory and the various techniques by which materials are examined for age, condition and authenticity.

Gettens, Rutherford J. "European Conservation Laboratories," *Museum News,* 39:4 (December 1960), pp. 23-27.

Hall, E.T. "Methods of Analysis (Physical and Microchemical) Applied to Paintings and Antiquities." In *Recent Advances in Conservation* (London: Butterworths, 1963), pp. 29–32. ◆ Discusses comparative merits of various types of analytical procedure: standard wet chemistry; optical emission spectrometry; x-ray fluorescent spectrometry; x-ray diffraction; electron probe microanalyser.

Hanlan, J.F. "The EDX Spectrometer in Museum Use," *Bulletin of the American Group—IIC,* 11:2 (April 1971), pp. 85–90.

Hanson, Victor F. "The Curator's Dream Instrument." In *Application of Science in the Examination of Works of Art; Proceedings of* *the Seminar: June 15–19, 1970* (Boston: Museum of Fine Arts, 1973), pp. 18–30. ◆ Discusses energy dispersive x-ray fluorescence analysis identification of maker, date, place, method, material.

Hodges, H.W.M. "Equipping the Laboratory—Basic Equipment and Processes." In *The Conservation of Cultural Property with Special Reference to Tropical Conditions* (Paris: UNESCO, 1968). pp. 80–90.

International Centre for the Study of the Preservation and the Restoration of Cultural Property. *International Inventory of the Museum Laboratories and Restoration Workshops.* Works and Publications no. 1. Rome: The Centre, with the cooperation of the International Council of Museums, 1960. 274 pp.

Johnson, B.B. "The Conservation Center of the Los Angeles County Museum of Art." In *IIC—American Group Technical Papers from 1968 through 1970* (New York: IIC-AG, 1970), pp. 103–108.

Keck, Caroline. "On Conservation: Equipment Needed for Elementary Care," *Museum News,* 50:4 (December 1971), p. 13.

Oddy, W.A., and H. Barker. "A Feature Card Information-Retrieval System for the General Museum Laboratory," *Studies in Conservation,* 16:3 (August 1971), pp. 89–94.

Organ, R.M. *Design for Scientific Conservation of Antiquities.* Washington, D.C.: Smithsonian Institution Press, 1969. 497 pp., photos, drawings, diagrams, graphs, tables, equipment and supply source lists, bibliog , index. ◆ Discusses equipment, tools, layout of laboratory, sources of supply.

Quandt, Eleanor S. "Insurance in the Conservation Laboratory, Part II," *Bulletin of the American Group—IIC,* 1:1 (1961), pp. 7–9.

Robertson, Clements L. "A Museum Conservation Laboratory," *Museum News,* 43:5 (January 1965), pp. 15–21.

Robertson, Clements L. "The Visual and Optical Examination of Works of Art," *Museum News,* 46:4 (December 1967), Technical Supplement no. 20.

Stolow, Nathan. "Problems in Setting up a Museum Laboratory." In *Application of Science in the Examination of Works of Art; Proceedings of the Seminar: September 15–18, 1958* (Boston: Museum of Fine Arts, 1959), pp. 1–16.

United Nations Educational, Scientific and Cultural Organization. *UNESCO Source Book for Science Teaching.* 2nd ed., rev., 24th imprint. Paris: UNESCO, 1970. 250 pp., illus., tables, paperback. ◆ Includes a section on how to build balances and other lab equipment out of junk.

Walden, T.A. "Laboratories and Workshops—Museums," *Museums Journal,* 63:1–2 (June–September, 1963), pp. 70–73.

Werner, A.E.A. "The British Museum Research Laboratory," *Museums Journal,* 62:3 (December 1962), pp. 153–159.

4

Training of Conservators

As stated in the preceding chapter, there are not enough conservators with professional training although such training is the foundation on which the profession must necessarily rest. This need has given rise to a number of programs and training centers in the United States, Canada and Europe.

The first section of this chapter cites general references to these efforts. Then, details of specific programs are described with information on the course of study, entrance requirements, and degrees awarded.

"Basic Minimum Standards for Training Paper Conservators by the Apprenticeship System: A Proposal," *Bulletin of the American Group—IIC,* 11:2 (April 1971), pp. 1–7.

Calouste Gulbenkian Foundation. Committee to Consider the Establishment of an Institute for Training in the Conservation of Paintings and Drawings. *Training in the Conservation of Paintings.* London: The Foundation, 1972. 100 pp., appendices. ◆ Lists and describes most of the training programs in painting conservation. Directed primarily at the British Government, but implications, analyses and conclusions are of interest to an international audience. Available from the Calouste Gulbenkian Foundation, 98 Portland Place, London, England.

Cannon-Brookes, Peter. "Conservation and the Training of Art Museum Staff," *Museums Journal,* 72:4 (March 1973), pp. 146–148.

Coremans, Paul. "The Training of Restorers." In *Problems of Conservation in Museums* (Paris: Editions Eyrolles, 1969), pp. 7–32. ◆ Includes historical survey; treatment of museum objects; training centers; recruitment.

Hodges, Henry. "An Ab Initio Course in the Conservation of Antiquities." In *Recent Advances in Conservation* (London: Butterworths, 1963), pp. 211–213.

Hodges, Henry W. "Training in Conservation," *Museums Journal,* 61:3 (December 1961), pp. 203–204.

Keck, Sheldon. "1st Aid for Art," *Museum News,* 43:1 (September 1964), pp. 13–17. ◆ Describes conservation training course at New York University Institute of Fine Arts.

Keck, Sheldon. "A Little Training Can Be a Dangerous Thing," *Museum News,* 52:4 (December 1973), pp. 40–42. ◆ Advocates extended course in curatorial conservation responsibilities in regular museum training programs.

Keck, Sheldon. "Training for Engineers in Conservation." In *Recent Advances in Conservation* (London: Butterworths, 1963), pp. 199–201.

Pratt, Peter. "Curricula for Conservation Learning and Teaching in England and Turkey," *Bulletin of APT,* 3:1 (1971), pp. 22–29.

Ruhemann, Helmut. "The Training of Restorers." In *Recent Advances in Conservation* (London: Butterworths, 1963), pp. 203–205.

Wennberg, Bo, and Gunnar Schiller. "The Training of Restorers in Denmark, Finland, Norway, and Sweden." In *Problems of Conservation in Museums* (Paris: Editions Eyrolles, 1969), pp. 63–68.

Training Programs

Art Conservation Department, University of Delaware, Newark, Delaware 19711.

The Art Conservation Program was established in 1974 as a joint effort between the H. F. duPont Winterthur Museum and the University of Delaware and accepts ten students per year. The three year course consists of two years of study and practical work at the University of Delaware and the Winterthur Museum followed by a one year internship with a conservator of professional qualifications in a conservation department laboratory, or studio.

MINIMUM ADMISSION REQUIREMENTS: Bachelor of Arts Degree in either art history, archaeology or anthropology, studio art or chemistry plus a strong minor concentration in the disciplines of art history, chemistry, and studio art. Applicants with degrees in other majors will be considered if they also have good backgrounds in art history, chemistry, and studio art.

AWARD: Master of Science Degree in the Conservation of Artistic and Historic Objects.

Canadian Conservation Institute Conservator Training Program, National Museums of Canada, Ottawa, K1A OM8, Canada.

The CCI Conservator Training Program was established in 1973 and discontinued in 1976. While in operation it accepted ten students per year. The three year course consisted of two years of classes and work projects at the CCI headquarters, followed by a year of internship at another institution.

REQUIREMENTS: University graduation (Honours degree) with concentration in one of the following fields: history of art, studio art, archeology, history, anthropology, ethnology, museology, chemistry and physics. All applicants were required to have at least one year of chemistry.

AWARD: Upon completion of the Program, graduates qualified for a position as Assistant Conservator in the CCI, other federal museums or departments, or in provincial, municipal or private museums.

Center for Conservation and Technical Studies, Fogg Art Museum, Cambridge, Massachusetts 02138.

The Fogg Art Museum Conservation Program was established in 1973 and accepts two students per year. The program consists of a three year apprenticeship or a one year internship under established conservators.

REQUIREMENTS (apprenticeship): B.A. degree with a strong background in history of art, at least one college level chemistry course, studio art experience and competence in one foreign language.

REQUIREMENTS (internship): Same as for apprenticeship plus at least two years of formal experience in the field.

AWARD: Certificate from the Fogg Art Museum.

Conservation Centre of the Institute of Fine Arts, New York University, James B. Duke House, Fifth Avenue and 78th Street, New York, New York 10021.

The Conservation Centre of the Institute of Fine Arts Training Program was established in 1960 and accepts four students per year. The course is three years for those who already have a Master's degree in History of Art and four years for those who do not have a Master's degree. The major specialized course of the final two years starts with a one year internship in the conservation department or laboratory of a museum or gallery in the United States or abroad. The last year is spent on practical work at the Centre.

REQUIREMENTS: B.A. in History of Art plus courses in the physical sciences and a demonstrated ability in studio art.

AWARD: Diploma in conservation.

Conservation of Historic and Artistic Works, Cooperstown Graduate Programs, State University College at Oneonta, Cooperstown, New York 13326.

The Cooperstown Graduate Program in the Conservation of Historic and Artistic Works was established in 1970 and accepts ten students per year. The three year course consists of two years of study and practical work at Cooperstown, followed by a one year internship in some other conservation laboratory.

REQUIREMENTS: Bachelor of Arts degree or its equivalent from an accredited college or art school with a major in history of art, studio art, or chemistry; a minor in a second of these; and course work in a third.

AWARD: Master of Arts degree and certificate of advanced study in the Conservation of Historic and Artistic Works.

The Courtauld Institute of Art—Technology Department, Home House, 20 Portman Square, London, England.

The Courtauld Institute of Art training program was established in 1965 and accepts two students per year. The two year course consists of class work and practical work in the Department.

REQUIREMENTS: Students must be graduates or the equivalent (e.g., Dip. A.D.) in art, art history, or the natural sciences.

AWARD: Certificate.

The Intermuseum Conservation Association Training Program, Intermuseum Laboratory, Allen Art Building, Oberlin, Ohio 44074.

The Intermuseum Conservation Association Training Program was established in 1970. It is now being phased out and accepted its last class of three students in September 1975. The three year course consists of work in the Intermuseum Conservation Laboratory and independent projects at other institutions.

REQUIREMENTS: B.A. degree including courses in art history, chemistry and studio art; and manual dexterity.

AWARD: Certificate of competence.

International Centre for the Study of the Preservation and the Restoration of Cultural Property, Training Section, 13 Via di San Michele, 00153, Rome, Italy. U.S. citizens request forms from: International Centre Committee, c/o The Executive Director, Advisory Council on Historic Preservation, Suite 430, 1522 K Street, N.W., Washington, D.C. 20005.

The International Centre offers three training courses.

Architectural Conservation includes lectures on the theory and methodology of architectural conservation as well as research, practical application, discussions and seminars. Conservation is considered from the points of view of the individual building, the material used, and the environment of which it is a part.

The course is open to architects, civil engineers, urban designers, archeologists, and art historians with university degrees. It is held each year from January to June. Lectures are held in English, French and Italian, with simultaneous translations into English and whenever possible and necessary, into French.

Conservation of Mural Paintings is a course of training organized by the Centre and placed under the scientific direction of the Instituto Centrale del Restauro in agreement with the Italian Antiquities and Fine Arts Department. It is an introduction to specialization in the technological examination and the preservation of mural paintings. Participants will be offered a systematic approach to problems, up-to-date theories and methods, practical demonstrations and field work.

The course is intended for restorers of paintings holding a diploma or having professional experience of at least three years. It is held each year from March to July. Lectures are given in French in odd years, in English in even years.

Fundamental Principles of Conservation is a course designed to explain, with the aid of demonstrations and exercises, the structure of materials and their deterioration processes, the products used in conservation, and the rules governing all conservation processes.

The course is intended for all types of specialists in the preservation of cultural property, with special reference to objects of historic and artistic interest. It is held each year from January to April. The official language of the course is English.

NOTES

Calouste Gulbenkian Foundation, Lisbon. United Kingdom and British Commonwealth Branch, 98 Portland Place, London W1N 4ET, England. In 1969 the Calouste Gulbenkian Foundation set up and financed a Committee of Inquiry to investigate the problem of the conservation of Britain's paintings and drawings. This committee recommended the establishment of an Institute for Training in the Conservation of Paintings and Drawings. The Foundation offered £150,000 toward the establishment of such an institute, provided the balance of costs could be found by the British Government, or some other source. This proposal is still under discussion.

5

Environmental Factors in Conservation

Professional conservators, as well as some administrators and curators, understand and appreciate the significance of environmental factors in the care of works of art. Only recently, however, have most laymen and nonspecialists come to realize the dangers inherent in inadequate collections care.

What officers, trustees, collectors, and even the general public must understand is that all works of art are doomed unless they are given optimum protection from the inevitable dangers that beset them. The adverse effects of excessive light and fluctuating humidities have always been present, but our industrial age has raised other damaging spectres: air pollution, vibrations, and artificial environments. And to those dangers must be added fire, insect damage, risk of theft and vandalism, the effects of accident, and of travel and transport. The list sometimes seems endless.

Environment is the area in which the layperson and the specialist can join to take positive actions to assure the survival of their materials and objects. Environmental control has been called the preventive medicine of conservation. If the conditions under which works of art are exhibited, stored or transported are adverse, all the efforts of conservators are to no avail. In this chapter are the references that will enable individuals and organizations to set up an effective collections care program.

General Considerations

Boustead, William. "The Conservation of Works of Art in Tropical and Sub-Tropical Zones." In *Recent Advances in Conservation* (London: Butterworths, 1963), pp. 73–78.

Brommelle, Norman S. "Conservation of Museum Objects in the Tropics." In *Contributions to the London Conference on Museum Climatology* (London: International Institute for Conservation of Historic and Artistic Works, 1968), pp. 139–149.

Brommelle, Norman S. "Lighting, Air-Conditioning, Exhibition, Storage, Handling, and Packing." In *The Conservation of Cultural Property with Special Reference to Tropical Conditions* (Paris: UNESCO, 1968), pp. 291–303.

Brawne, Michael. "Museum Design for Conservation." In *Contributions to the London Conference on Museum Climatology* (London: International Institute for Conservation of Historic and Artistic Works, 1968), pp. 75–78.

Buck, Richard D. "The Inspection of Collections," *Museum News,* 29:7 (October 1, 1951), pp. 6–8. ◆ A system for recording condition.

Buck, Richard D. "On Conservation: The Energy Crisis and Museum Collections," *Museum News,* 52:7 (April 1974), pp. 8–9. ◆ Discusses air pollution, lighting, heating and air conditioning, temperature and relative humidity.

Cameron, Duncan. "Environmental Control: A Theoretical Solution," *Museum News,* 46:9 (May 1968), pp. 17–21.

23

Church of England. Council of Diocesan Advisory Committee for the Care of Churches. *How to Protect a Church in War-Time; the Care of Churches and Church Goods under War Conditions.* 3rd ed., rev. London: A.R. Mowbray & Co., Ltd. (for the Council), 1940. 31 pp.

"Climatology and Conservation in Museums," *Museums,* XIII:4 (1960), entire issue.

Coremans, Paul. "Climate and Microclimate." In *The Conservation of Cultural Property with Special Reference to Tropical Conditions* (Paris: UNESCO, 1968), pp. 27–39.

Douglas, R.A. "A Common Sense Approach to Environmental Control," *Curator,* XV: 2 (June 1972), pp. 139–144.

Drew, Jane B. "Museum Design with Special Reference to the Tropics." In *Contributions to the London Conference on Museum Climatology* (London: International Institute for Conservation of Historic and Artistic Works, 1968), pp. 183–189.

Dunn, Walter S., Jr. "Storing Your Collections: Problems and Solutions," rev. ed., *History News,* 25:6 (June 1970), Technical Leaflet no. 5 (new series).

Graham, John, II, and the Curatorial Department of Colonial Williamsburg. "Solving Storage Problems," *Museum News,* 41:4 (December 1962), pp. 24–29.

International Centre for the Study of the Preservation and the Restoration of Cultural Property. *Climatology and Conservation in Museums.* Rome: The Centre, 1960. 289 pp., illus., diagrams, bibliog. ◆ In French and English. Published with the cooperation of UNESCO and ICOM.

International Institute for Conservation of Historic and Artistic Works. *Control of the Museum Environment: A Basic Summary.* London: The Institute, 1967. 8 pp. ◆ Based on the findings of the 1967 London Conference on Museum Climatology.

Jedrzejewska, Hanna. "Damaging Influence of Disinfecting Agents on Sensitive Ancient Materials." In *Contributions to the London Conference on Museum Climatology* (London: International Institute for Conservation of Historic and Artistic Works, 1968), pp. 95–101.

Jones, E.H. "The Problems of Venice." In *IIC—American Group Technical Papers from 1968 through 1970* (New York: IIC-AG, 1970), pp. 15–20.

Keck, Caroline K. "Conservation: Security Depends on People," *History News,* 29:4 (April 1974), pp. 79, 94. ◆ Instructions on how to close an historic house.

Keck, Caroline K. *Safeguarding Your Collection in Travel.* Nashville, Tenn.: American Association for State and Local History, 1970. 78 pp., illus. ◆ Provides instructions for pre-shipment inspection, packing, transporting and insurance. Illustrations show procedures for making photographic records and solving specific packing problems.

Kimberly, Arthur E., and J.F.G. Hicks, Jr. *A Survey of Storage Conditions in Libraries Relative to the Preservation of Records.* U.S. Bureau of Standards Miscellaneous Publication no. 128. Washington, D.C.: U.S. Government Printing Office, 1931. 8 pp., tables.

Lanier, Mildred B. "Storage Facilities at Colonial Williamsburg," *Museum News,* 45:6 (February 1967), pp. 31–33.

London Conference on Museum Climatology. *Contributions to the London Conference on Museum Climatology, 18–23 September, 1967.* Edited by Garry Thomson. London: International Institute for Conservation of Historic and Artistic Works, 1968. 296 pp., illus., bibliog. references, paperback. ◆ A study of how the environment in a museum affects its contents and how to ensure that their inevitable ageing processes are slowed.

Michaels, Peter. "Lender Beware," *Museum News,* 43:1 (September 1964), pp. 11–12.

Padfield, Tim. "Design of Museum Showcases." In *Contributions to the London Conference on Museum Climatology* (London: International Institute for Conservation of Historic and Artistic Works, 1968), pp. 119–126.

Plenderleith, Harold J., and P. Philippot. "Climatologie and Conservation in Museums," *Museum,* XXII:4 (1960), pp. 242–289.

Pomerantz, Louis. "Art Consumption," *Museum News,* 49:3 (November 1970), pp. 10–11. ◆ Editorial comment on loans by art museums.

"Solving Storage Problems," *Museum News,* 41:4 (December 1962), pp. 24–29.

Stansfield, G. *Physical Storage of Museum Reserve Collections.* London: Museums Association, 1971. 3 pp.

Stout, George L. "Preservation of Paintings in War-Time," *Technical Studies in the Field of the Fine Arts,* X:3 (January 1942), pp. 161–172.

Sugden, Robert P. *Care and Handling of Art Objects.* New York: Metropolitan Museum of Art, 1946. 32 pp., illus., bibliog. ◆ Summary of instructions for the care and handling of art objects including paintings, large and small objects, textiles and works of art on paper. Intended to establish certain fundamental rules for the protection of objects in motion.

Torraca, Giorgio. "Deterioration Processes of Mural Paintings." In *Application of Science in the Examination of Works of Art; Proceedings of the Seminar: June 15–19, 1970* (Boston: Museum of Fine Arts, 1973), pp. 170–175.

Trewartha, Glenn T. *An Introduction to Climate.* 4th ed. New York: McGraw-Hill, Inc., 1968. 408 pp., illus., maps, bibliog. ◆ Previous editions published under title: *An Introduction to Weather and Climate.*

United Nations Educational, Scientific and Cultural Organization. *Report on the Draft Recommendation to Member States Concerning the Preservation of Cultural Property Endangered by Public or Private Works.* Document SHc/4. Paris: UNESCO, 1967. various pagings, addenda 1–2.

United Nations Educational, Scientific and Cultural Organization. *Technical and Legal Aspects of the Preparation of International Regulations to Prevent the Illicit Export, Import and Sale of Cultural Property.* Paris: UNESCO, 1962. 11 pp.

U.S. Library of Congress. General Reference and Bibliography Division. *Safeguarding Our Cultural Heritage: A Bibliography on the Protection of Museums, Works of Art, Monuments, Archives, and Libraries in Time of War.* Compiled by Nelson R. Burr. Washington, D.C.: Library of Congress, 1952. 117 pp.

Waddell, Gene. "Museum Storage," *Museum News,* 49:5 (January 1971), pp. 14–20.

Wessel, Carl J. "Environmental Factors Affecting the Permanence of Library Materials," *Library Quarterly,* 40:1 (January 1970), pp. 39–84.

Air Conditioning

Amdur, Elias J. "Humidity Control—Isolated Area Plan," *Museum News,* 43:4 (December 1964), Technical Supplement no. 5.

Bockwijt, W.O., and B.H. Vos. "Measuring Method for Determining Moisture Content and Moisture Distribution in Monuments," *Studies in Conservation,* 15:2 (May 1970), pp. 81–93.

Boustead, William M. "Dehumidification in Museum Storage Areas." In *Contributions to the London Conference on Museum Climatology* (London: International Institute for Conservation of Historic and Artistic Works, 1968), pp. 103–107.

Buck, Richard D. "A Specification for Museum Air Conditioning," *Museum News,* 43:4 (December 1964), Technical Supplement no. 5.

Carson, Frederick T. *Effect of Humidity on Physical Properties of Paper.* Washington, D.C.: U.S. Government Printing Office, 1944. 12 pp., tables, diagrams, references.

Cursiter, Stanley. "Control of Air in Cases and Frames," *Technical Studies in the Field of the Fine Arts,* V:2 (October 1936), pp. 109–116.

DeBoer, J.R.J. Van Asperen. "Humidity in Walls in Relation to the Preservation of Works of Art." In *Contributions to the London Conference on Museum Climatology* (London: International Institute for Conservation of Historic and Artistic Works, 1968), pp. 109–117.

Garver, Thomas H. "Control of Atmospheric Pollutants and Maintenance of Stable Climatic Conditions." In *Contributions to the London Conference on Museum Climatology* (London: International Institute for Conservation of Historic and Artistic Works, 1968), pp. 23–27.

Haagen-Smit, A.J. "Air Pollution and Preservation of Art." In *IIC–American Group Technical Papers from 1968 through 1970* (New York: IIC-AG, 1970), pp. 5–14.

Haagen-Smit, A.J. "The Chemistry of Atmospheric Pollution." In *Contributions to the London Conference on Museum Climatology* (London: International Institute for Conservation of Historic and Artistic Works, 1968), pp. 89–93.

Harvey, John. "Air Conditioning for

Museums," *Museums Journal*, 73:1 (June 1973), pp. 11–16.

Hochkeiser, S. *Methods of Measuring and Monitoring Atmospheric Sulphur Dioxide.* Cincinnati, Ohio: U.S. Department of Health, Education and Welfare, Public Health Service, 1964. 47 pp., bibliog.

Howorth, F. Hugh. "An Approach to Air Conditioning." In *Contributions to the London Conference on Museum Climatology* (London: International Institute for Conservation of Historic and Artistic Works, 1968), pp. 173–182.

International Congress on Air Pollution, 1st, New York, 1955. *Problems and Control of Air Pollution.* Proceedings of the First International Congress on Air Pollution held in New York City, March 1–2, 1955. New York: Reinhold Publishing Corp., 1955. 272 pp., illus., maps, bibliog.

Keally, F., and Henry C. Meyer. "Air-Conditioning as a Means of Preserving Books and Records," *The American Archivist*, 12:3 (July 1949), pp. 280–282.

Keck, Caroline K. "On Conservation: Relative Humidity Controls," *Museum News*, 50:8 (April 1972), p. 13.

Kimberly, Arthur E., and Adelaide L. Emley. *A Study of the Removal of Sulphur Dioxide from Library Air.* Issued October 17, 1933. Washington, D.C.: U.S. Government Printing Office, 1933. 9 pp., illus., tables, diagrams. ◆ U.S. National Bureau of Standards Miscellaneous Publications No. 142.

Kühn, Hermann. "The Effect of Oxygen, Relative Humidity and Temperature on the Fading Rate of Water Colours." In *Contributions to the London Conference on Museum Climatology* (London: International Institute for Conservation of Historic and Artistic Works, 1968), pp. 79–88.

Kühn, Hermann. "The Use of Heat-Protection Filters When Works of Art Are Filmed or Televised," *Studies in Conservation*, 12:3 (August 1967), pp. 102–116.

Leithe, Wolfgang. *The Analysis of Air Pollutants.* Translated by R. Kondor. Ann Arbor, Mich.: Ann Arbor Science Publishers, 1970. 304 pp., illus., bibliog.

Lewis, L. Logan. "Air Conditioning for Museums," *Museum*, X:2 (1957), pp. 132–147.

McCrone, Walter C., and John Gustav Delly. *The Particle Atlas Edition Two. An Encyclopedia of Techniques for Small Particle Identification.* Ann Arbor, Mich.: Ann Arbor Science Publishers, Inc., 1973. 4 vols., illus. ◆ Vol. 1: *Principles, Instrumentation and Techniques;* Vol. 2: *Light Microscopy Atlas;* Vol. 3: *Electron Microscopy Atlas;* Vol. 4: *Handbook for Analysts.*

McCrone, Walter C., and Ronald Draftz. "The Importance of Thinking Small," *Heating, Piping and Air Conditioning*, 37 (January 1966), pp. 126–133. ◆ Analysis and identification of microscopic contaminants.

McCrone, Walter C.; Ronald G. Draftz; and John Gustav Delly. *The Particle Atlas; A Photomicrographic Reference for the Microscopical Identification of Particulate Substances.* Ann Arbor, Mich.: Ann Arbor Science Publishers, 1967. 406 pp., illus., bibliog.

Massari, Giovanni, and Paolo Mora. "Dampness and the Preservation of Mural Paintings." In *Contributions to the London Conference on Museum Climatology* (London: International Institute for Conservation of Historic and Artistic Works, 1968), pp. 191–198.

Meetham, A.R. *Atmospheric Pollution—Its Origins and Prevention.* 3rd rev. ed. Oxford: Pergamon Press, Ltd., 1964. 301 pp., illus., bibliog.

Organ, R.M. "Humidification of Galleries for a Temporary Exhibition." In *Contributions to the London Conference on Museum Climatology* (London: International Institute for Conservation of Historic and Artistic Works, 1968), pp. 1–13.

Padfield, Tim. "The Control of Relative Humidity and Air Pollution in Showcases and Picture Frames," *Studies in Conservation*, 11:1 (February 1966), pp. 8–30.

Severns, William H., and Julian R. Fellows. *Air Conditioning and Refrigeration.* New York: John Wiley & Sons, Inc., 1958. 563 pp., illus.

Stevens, W.C. "Rates of Change in the Dimension and Moisture Contents of Wooden Panels Resulting from Changes in the Ambient Air Conditions," *Studies in Conservation*, 6:1 (February 1961), pp. 21–25.

Stolow, Nathan. "The Action of Environment on Museum Objects, Part I: Humidity, Temperature, Atmospheric Pollution," *Curator,* IX:3 (September 1966), pp. 175–185.

Stolow, Nathan. "Environmental Security." In *A Primer on Museum Security* (Cooperstown, N.Y.: New York State Historical Association, 1966), pp. 39–50.

Stolow, Nathan. "Fundamental Case Design for Humidity Sensitive Collections," *Museum News,* 44:6 (February 1966), Technical Supplement no. 11. ◆ Discusses problems and solutions to maintaining environmental stability in a packing case or exhibition case.

Thring, Meredith W., ed. *Air Pollution; Based on Papers Given at a Conference at the University of Sheffield, September 1956.* London: Butterworths Scientific Pub., 1957. 248 pp., illus., maps, charts, diagrams, tables, bibliog.

Toishi, Kenzo. "Relative Humidity in a Closed Package." In *Recent Advances in Conservation* (London: Butterworths, 1963), pp. 13–15.

Vos, B.H. "Suction of Ground Water," *Studies in Conservation,* 16:4 (November 1971), pp. 129–144. ◆ The height of rise of water in walls is determined mainly by the relative humidity of the ambient air; methods to prevent water rising in walls are discussed.

Waller, R.E. "Studies on the Nature of Urban Air Pollution," In *Contributions to the London Conference on Museum Climatology* (London: International Institute for Conservation of Historic and Artistic Works, 1968), pp. 65–69.

Light

Balder, J.J. *The Discoloration of Colored Objects Under the Influence of Daylight, Incandescent Lamplight and Fluorescent Lamplight.* Leiden: The Netherlands Museum Association, 1956. 48 pp., illus., bibliog. ◆ A comparison of the fading and discoloring effects of various light sources.

Crawford, B.H. "Colour Rendition and Museum Lighting," *Studies in Conservation,* 5:2 (May 1969), pp. 41–51.

Demeny, L. "Degradation of Cotton Yarns by Light from Fluorescent Lamps." In *Contributions to the London Conference on Museum Climatology* (London: International Institute for Conservation of Historic and Artistic Works, 1968), pp. 53–64.

Feller, Robert L. "Control of Deteriorating Effects of Light on Museum Objects: Heating Effects of Illumination by Incandescent Lamps," *Museum News,* 46:9 (May 1968), Technical Supplement. ◆ A study on the effect of light, oxygen, and other factors on the deterioration of paint and organic materials, and methods and materials for overcoming it.

Feller, Robert L. "Control of Deteriorating Effects of Light Upon Museum Objects," *Museum,* XVII:2 (1964), entire issue.

Feller, Robert L. "The Deteriorating Effects of Light on Museum Objects," *Museum News,* 42:10 (June 1964), Technical Supplement no. 3.

Hall, E.T. "An Ultraviolet Monitor for Museums." In *Contributions to the London Conference on Museum Climatology* (London: International Institute for Conservation of Historic and Artistic Works, 1968), pp. 151–158.

Hanlan, J.F. "The Effect of Electronic Photographic Lamps on the Materials of Works of Art," *Museum News,* 48:10 (June 1970), Technical Supplement.

Harris, J.B. "Practical Aspects of Lighting as Related to Conservation." In *Contributions to the London Conference on Museum Climatology* (London: International Institute for Conservation of Historic and Artistic Works, 1968), pp. 133–138.

Harrison, Laurence S. "Evaluation of Spectral Radiation Hazards in Window-Lighted Galleries." In *Recent Advances in Conservation* (London: Butterworths, 1963), pp. 1–6.

Harrison, Laurence S. *Report on the Deteriorating Effects of Modern Light Sources.* New York: The Metropolitan Museum of Art, 1954. 20, 17 pp., diagrams, tables. ◆ Very important seminal work on the effects of light on museum objects. Out-of-print.

Illuminating Engineering Society, London. *Lighting of Art Galleries and Museums.* Illuminating Engineering Society Technical Report 14. London: The Society, 1970. 33 pp., illus. ◆ Available from the Illuminating Engineering Society, York House, Westminster Bridge Road, London SE 1, England.

Keck, Caroline K. "On Conservation: Converting Fluorescent Lighting in Museum Cases," *Museum News,* 50:7 (March 1972), p. 13.

Lodewijks, J. "The Influence of Light on Museum Objects." In *Recent Advances in Conservation* (London: Butterworths, 1963), pp. 7–8.

Padfield, Tim. "A Simple Ultraviolet Radiation Detector for Museum Use," *Studies in Conservation,* 12:1 (February 1967), pp. 1–4.

Stolow, Nathan. "The Action of Environment on Museum Objects, Part II: Light," *Curator,* IX:4 (December 1966), pp. 298–306.

Stolow, Nathan. "Light and Its Effect on Museum Objects." In *A Primer on Museum Security* (Cooperstown, N.Y.: New York State Historical Association, 1966), pp. 50–58.

Thompson, Colin. "Daylight in Art Galleries," *Museums Journal,* 71:2 (September 1971), pp. 59–62.

Thomson, Garry. "Annual Exposure to Light Within Museums," *Studies in Conservation,* 12:1 (February 1967), pp. 26–35. ◆ How to estimate the annual exposure to light within museums from data on daylight variations combined with measurement of the quantity of light which reaches the wall.

Thomson, Garry. "Calibration and Use of an Ultraviolet Monitor." In *Contributions to the London Conference on Museum Climatology* (London: International Institute for Conservation of Historic and Artistic Works, 1968), pp. 159–172.

Thomson, Garry. *Conservation and Museum Lighting.* London: Museums Association, 1970. 6 pp.

Thomson, Garry. "A New Look at Colour Rendering, Level of Illumination and Protection from Ultraviolet Radiation in Museum Lighting," *Studies in Conservation,* 6:2 & 3 (August 1961), pp. 49–70.

Wolters, Christian, and Hermann Kühn. "Behavior of Painted Wood Panels Under Strong Illumination," *Studies in Conservation,* 7:1 (February 1962), pp. 1–9.

ducted by Gage-Babcock & Associates, Inc. Chicago: Library Technology Project, American Library Association, 1963. 322 pp., illus., bibliog. ◆ Reviews the types of physical losses in libraries, primarily by fire, and presents procedures and equipment for preventing fires and other forms of damage.

Chapman, Joseph. "Fire," *Museum News,* 50:5 (January 1972), pp. 32–35.

"Hot, Hotter, Hottest," *The Laboratory,* 34:3 (1966), pp. 66–70. ◆ A general discussion of the newest fire fighting materials.

National Fire Protection Association, Committee on Libraries, Museums, and Historic Buildings. *Protecting Our Heritage: A Discourse on Fire Prevention in Historic Buildings and Landmarks.* 2nd ed. Edited by Joseph F. Jenkins. Boston: National Fire Protection Association, with the assistance of the American Association for State and Local History, 1970. 39 pp., photos, appendices, glossary of fire protection equipment, paperback. ◆ Suggests precautions which should be taken in historic buildings to prevent fires and to deal with fire emergencies if they occur. Available from National Fire Protection Association, 60 Batterymarch Street, Boston, Massachusetts 02110, or from the American Association for State and Local History, 1400 Eighth Avenue South, Nashville, Tennessee 37203.

Windeler, Peter. "Fire: Endangers the Past— for the Future," *Museums Journal,* 70:2 (September 1970), pp. 72–74.

NOTES

Sonalarm Signal System. Cole-Parmer Instrument Company, 7425 North Oak Park Avenue, Chicago, Illinois 60648. The Sonalarm Signal System is recommended by the American Institute for Conservation of Historic and Artistic Works for protecting valuable contents of cabinets. Any temperature rise is indicated by alternate flashing lights and a repeating audio signal warning.

Fire Protection

American Library Association, Library Technology Project. *Protecting the Library and its Resources: A Guide to Physical Protection and Insurance.* Report on a Study Con-

Insect Control

Brown, Anthony W.A. *Insect Control by Chemicals.* New York: John Wiley, 1951. 817 pp., illus., diagrams, bibliog.

Deschiens, Robert, and Christine Coste. "Protection of Works of Art in Carved Wood from Attacks of Wood-Eating Insects," *Museum,* X:1 (1957), pp. 55–59.

Hickin, Norman E. *The Insect Factor in Wood Decay; An Account of Wood Boring Insects with Particular Reference to Timber Indoors.* 2nd ed. London: Hutchinson & Co., 1968. 344 pp., illus., map, bibliog.

Marshall, Morgan. "The Termite Menace," *Technical Studies in the Field of the Fine Arts,* IV:3 (January 1936), pp. 127–134.

Metcalf, Clell Lee, and Wesley P. Flint. *Destructive and Useful Insects: Their Habits and Control.* 4th ed. New York: McGraw-Hill Book Co., 1962. 1087 pp., illus.

Szent-Ivany, J.J.H. "Identification and Control of Insect Pests." In *The Conservation of Cultural Property with Special Reference to Tropical Conditions* (Paris: UNESCO, 1968), pp. 53–70. ◆ Includes identification and control of bristle-tails, crickets, grasshoppers, cockroaches, mantids, termites, booklice, butterflies, moths, ants, wasps, bees and beetles. Also includes a bibliography and an appendix on book insect repellents.

Weiss, H.B., and Ralph H. Carruthers. *Insect Enemies of Books.* New York: The New York Public Library, 1945. 63 pp., bibliog. ◆ Reprinted from the *Bulletin of the New York Public Library,* September–December, 1936.

Yadon, Vernal L. "A Portable Fumigation Chamber for the Small Museum," *Museum News,* 44:5 (January 1966), pp. 38–39.

PERIODICALS

Pesticide Handbook–Entoma. 1948, annual. Entomological Society of America, 4603 Calvert Road, P.O. Box AJ, College Park, Maryland 20740. ◆ Published every year except 1973. 1948–1972, published by the College Science Publishers; beginning 1974, published by Entomological Society.

Security

Bostick, William A. "What is the State of Museum Security?" *Museum News,* 46:5 (January 1968), pp. 13–19.

Carroll, Richard S. "A Low-Cost System of Protecting Paintings," *Museum News,* 41:10 (June 1963), pp. 27–29.

Chapman, Joseph. "Museum Security," *Museum News,* 50:1 (September 1971), pp. 43–45.

Chapman, Joseph. "Physical Security." In *A Primer on Museum Security* (Cooperstown, N.Y.: New York State Historical Association, 1966), pp. 1–14.

Chapman, Joseph. " . . . Stepping Up Security," *Museum News,* 44:3 (November 1965), pp. 18–21.

Chapman, Joseph. "Your Security Questions Answered," *Museum News,* 50:5 (January 1972), pp. 22–25.

Esterow, Milton. *The Art Stealers.* New York: Macmillan, 1966. 246 pp., photos, index.

Fitzsimons, Neal. "Emergency Measures and Museums," *Museum News,* 43:6 (February 1965), pp. 23–24.

Foramitti, Hans. "A Modern Approach to the Prevention of Thefts of Works of Art," *ICOM News,* 24:4 (December 1971), pp. 72–73.

Francis, Frank. "Security," *Museums Journal,* 63:1&2 (June–September 1963), pp. 28–32.

Gossin, Francis. "A Security Chief Comments on Guards," *Museum News,* 50:5 (January 1972), pp. 30–31.

Grossman, Albert J. "Television—Museum Watchdog," *Museum News,* 44:3 (November 1965), pp. 22–24.

Howard, Richard F. *Museum Security.* Washington, D.C.: American Association of Museums, 1958. 12 pp.

Katzive, David H. "Contemporary Art Loans, Trial By Fire," *Bulletin of the American Group—IIC,* 11:1 (October 1970), pp. 1–5.

Keck, Caroline K. "On Conservation: Vandalism," *Museum News,* 50:9 (May 1972), p. 9.

Keck, Caroline K. "Security Depends on People," *Curator,* X:1 (March 1967), pp. 54–59.

Keck, Caroline K.; Huntington T. Block; Joseph Chapman; John B. Lawton; and Nathan Stolow. *A Primer on Museum Security.* Cooperstown, N.Y.: New York State Historical Association, 1966. 85 pp., photos, graphs.

forms, bibliog., paperback. ◆ Contains basic information on physical security, insurance, environmental security, light and its effects on museum objects and other security factors.

McQuarie, Robert J. "Security," *Museum News*, 49:7 (March 1971), pp. 25–27.

Mannings, J. "Security of Museums and Art Galleries," *Museums Journal*, 70:1 (June 1970), pp. 7–9.

Michaels, A.F. "Security and the Museum," *Museum News*, 43:3 (November 1964), pp. 11–16.

Noblecourt, André F. "The Protection of Museums Against Theft," *Museum*, XVII:4 (1964), entire issue.

Pakalik, M.J. "Security and Protection in a Museum," *Curator*, I:4 (Autumn 1958), pp. 89–93.

Probst, Tom. "Electronic Eyes and Ears on Guard," *Museum News*, 44:3 (November 1965), pp. 11–17.

Rhoads, James B. "Alienation and Thievery: Archival Problems," *The American Archivist*, 29:2 (April 1966), pp. 197–208.

Schefrin, R.A. "Barriers to and Barriers of Library Security," *Wilson Library Bulletin*, 45:9 (May 1971), pp. 870–878.

Strickland, Robert L. "An Inexpensive Alarm System for the Small Museum," *Museum News*, 43:10 (June 1965), pp. 24–26.

Weldon, Stephen. "Winterthur: Security at a Decorative Arts Museum," *Museum News*, 50:5 (January 1972), pp. 36–37.

NOTES AND PERIODICALS

Burglary Protection Equipment List. Available from the Underwriters Laboratory, 207 East Ohio Street, Chicago, Illinois 60611.

Identifax Nationwide Registry, 1370 Avenue of the Americas, New York, New York 10019. Provides a nationwide computer registration system. Each member has an exclusive computerized code number which is registered on a data bank with his name, address, and telephone number. All law enforcement agencies have access to these records through a toll free telephone call. Yearly cost depends upon the number of items registered.

Security World: The Magazine of Professional Security Administration and Practice. 1964, monthly, subscription. Security World Publishing Company, 2639 South La Cienega Boulevard, Los Angeles, California 90034. ◆ Available on microfilm.

Packing and Shipping

Barail, Louis C. *Packaging Engineering.* New York: Reinhold Publishing Corp., 1954. 407 pp., illus.

Bauhof, W.A. "The Package Engineer in the Museum," *Museum News*, 44:4 (December 1965), pp. 27–28.

Beale, A. "Materials and Methods for the Packing and Handling of Ancient Metal Objects." In *IIC—American Group Technical Papers from 1968 through 1970* (New York: IIC-AG, 1970), pp. 89–96.

Brown, Kenneth. *Package Design Engineering.* New York: Wiley and Sons, 1959. 263 pp., illus.

Buck, Richard D. "Hazards of International Shipment," *Bulletin of the American Group—IIC*, 6 (May 1966), pp. 15–16.

Carmel, James H. *Exhibition Techniques—Travelling and Temporary.* New York: Reinhold Publishing Corporation, 1962. 216 pp., illus., bibliog. ◆ Includes sections on packaging and transport.

Fall, Frieda Kay. "New Industrial Packing Materials: Their Possible Uses for Museums," *Museum News*, 44:4 (December 1965), Technical Supplement no. 10.

Feller, Robert L. "Transportation of Panel Paintings by Courier in Winter." In *IIC—American Group Technical Papers from 1968 through 1970* (New York: IIC-AG, 1970), pp. 101–102.

Friedman, Walter, and Jerome Kipnees. *Industrial Packaging.* New York: Wiley & Sons, 1960. 536 pp., illus. ◆ Includes sections on corrugated and solid fibreboard, nailed wooden boxes and crates and wrapping, barrier and cushioning materials.

Gordon, James B. "Packing of Michelangelo's Pieta," *Studies in Conservation*, 12:2 (May 1967), pp. 57–69. ◆ Describes the shipment of the Pieta to the New York World's Fair, 1964–1965.

Hanft, W. "Packing for a Travelling Show of Prints," *Bulletin of the American Group—IIC,* 2:2 (April 1962), p. 12.

"Packing Paintings for Shipment," *Intermuseum Conservation Association Information Bulletin,* 4 (February 1958), pp. 1–2.

Roy Choudhury, Anil. *Art Museum Documentation and Practical Handling.* Hyderabad: Choudhury & Choudhury, 1963. 300 pp., illus., forms, bibliog. ♦ Includes a section on packing, handling and transportation.

Ruggles, Mervyn. "Transportation and Conservation of Twenty-Three Mural Paintings: An Exercise in Logistics and Preservation," *Bulletin of the American Institute for Conservation of Historic and Artistic Works,* 13:2 (1973), pp. 17–29.

Smith, Jack. "They Moved 500,000 Things and They Broke Only a Jar," *Museum News,* 43:10 (June 1965), pp. 19–23.

Speyers-Duran, Peter. *Moving Library Materials.* Rev. ed. Chicago: Library Technology Project, American Library Association, 1965. 63 pp., illus., bibliog.

Stolow, Nathan. *Controlled Environment for Works of Art in Transit.* London: Butterworths for the International Centre for the Study of the Preservation and the Restoration of Cultural Property, 1966. 46 pp., illus., tables, diagrams, bibliog., paperback. ♦ Available from Shoestring Press.

Stolow, Nathan, et al. *Report of the Working Group on the Care of Works of Art in Transit.* ICOM Committee for Conservation, Amsterdam, 15–19 September 1969. Amsterdam: ICOM Committee for Conservation, 1969. 30 pp., paperback.

Stolow, Nathan. "Some Studies on the Protection of Works of Art During Travel." In *Recent Advances in Conservation* (London: Butterworths, 1963), pp. 9–12.

Stolow, Nathan. "Standards of Care of Works of Art in Transit." In *Contributions to the London Conference on Museum Climatology* (London: International Institute for Conservation, 1968), pp. 271–284.

Stolow, Nathan. "The Technical Organization of an International Art Exhibition: Man and His World, Expo '67, Montreal," *Museum,* XXI:3 (1968), entire issue.

Toishi, Kenzo. " Jet Transport of Art Objects." In *Contributions to the London Conference on Museum Climatology* (London: International Institute for Conservation of Historic and Artistic Works, 1968), pp. 41–43.

Volkmer, J. "Special Problems in the Packing and Handling of Modern Art." In *IIC— American Group Technical Papers from 1968 through 1970* (New York: IIC-AG, 1970), pp. 97–100.

Wakefield, Hugh. "Methods of Packing in the Victoria and Albert Museum." In *Recent Advances in Conservation* (London: Butterworths, 1963), pp. 16–18.

Williamson, Moncrieff. "A Combination Shipping, Display and Storage Unit for Small Sculptures," *Museum News,* 41:6 (February 1963), pp. 34–36.

Flood and Water Damage

Amber, George H. *Water Damaged Files, Papers and Records: What to Do About Them.* Royal Oak, Mich.: Document Reclamation Service, Inc., 1963. 26 pp., illus., bibliog.

Fikioris, Margaret. *First Steps to be Taken for Emergency Treatment of Textiles.* Unpublished, on deposit at the New York State Historical Association Library, Cooperstown, New York, 1972. 2 pp., mimeo.

Horton, Carolyn. *Report and Recommendations on the Rescue of the Water-Damaged Books and Prints at the Corning Glass Center, Corning, New York, June 1972.* Unpublished, on deposit at the New York State Historical Association Library, Cooperstown, New York, 1972. 4 pp., supplies notes, mimeo.

Keck, Caroline K. "On Conservation: Instructions for Emergency Treatment of Water Damages," *Museum News,* 50:10 (June 1972), p. 13.

Keck, Sheldon. *Emergency Care of Museum Artifacts and Library Materials Affected by the Flood.* Unpublished, on deposit at the New York State Historical Association Library, Cooperstown, New York, 1972. 3 pp., mimeo.

Martin, Mervin. *Emergency Procedures for Furniture.* Unpublished, on deposit at the New York State Historical Association Library, Cooperstown, New York, 1972. 2 pp., recipes, mimeo.

Minogue, Adelaide. "Treatment of Fire and Water Damaged Records," *The American Archivist,* 9:1 (January 1946), pp. 17–25.

Montuori, Theodore. "Lesson Learned from Agnes." Reprinted from *The Journal of Micrographics,* 6:3 (January–February 1973), pp. 133–136.

Organ, Robert M., and Eleanor McMillan. "Aid to a Hurricane-Damaged Museum," *Bulletin of the American Group—IIC,* 10:1 (October 1969), pp. 31–39.

Rabin, Bernard. *Emergency Procedures for Musical Instruments.* Unpublished, on deposit at the New York State Historical Association Library, Cooperstown, New York, 1966. 1 p., mimeo.

Sellers, David Y., and Richard Strassberg. "Anatomy of a Library Emergency," *Library Journal,* 98:17 (October 1, 1973), pp. 2824–2827. ♦ How the Cornell University Libraries dealt with flood damage and developed plans to handle future emergencies.

Spawn, William. "After the Water Comes," Pennsylvania Library Association *Bulletin,* 28:6 (November 1973), pp. 242–251.

U.S. Department of Agriculture. *First Aid for Flooded Homes and Farms.* Agriculture Handbook No. 38. Washington, D.C.: U.S. Government Printing Office, 1972. 31 pp., photos, table, recipes, checklist, paperback. ♦ Useful notes for both historic houses and museums.

United States. Federal Fire Council. *Salvaging and Restoring Records Damaged by Fire and Water.* Recommended Practices #2. Washington, D.C.: Federal Fire Council, 1963. 17 pp., illus.

Waters, Peter. *Procedures for Salvage of Water-Damaged Library Materials.* Washington, D.C.: Library of Congress, 1975. 30 pp., sources of supplies, list of experts.

Waters, Peter, and The Royal College of Art. *The Restoration of Books, Florence 1968.* Film, 40 minutes, 16 mm., color, sound (1968). ♦ Shows types of damage, laboratories in Biblioteca Nazionale Centrale, and some excellent shots of binding techniques. May be used for television with proper credit to both the producer and the institution. Available from the Preservation Office, Library of Congress, Washington, D.C. 20540.

Weidner, Marilyn Kemp. *Instructions on How to Unframe Wet Prints.* Unpublished, on deposit at the New York State Historical Association Library, Cooperstown, New York, 1973. 4 pp., materials list, mimeo.

Whipkey, Harry E. *After Agnes: A Report on Flood Recovery Assistance by the Pennsylvania Historical and Museum Commission.* Harrisburg, Pa.: Pennsylvania Historical and Museum Commission, 1973. 23 pp., illus.

Mold and Fungus

Eastman Kodak Company. *Prevention and Removal of Fungus on Prints and Films.* Rochester, N.Y.: Eastman Kodak Company, 1971. 6 pp., pamphlet.

Gettens, Rutherford J.; Murray Pease; and George L. Stout. "The Problem of Mould Growth in Paintings," *Technical Studies in the Field of Fine Arts,* IX:3 (January 1941), pp. 127–144.

Hatch, Aram H. "Notes on the Experimental Studies Made for the Prevention of Mold Growth on Mural Paintings," *Technical Studies in the Field of the Fine Arts,* II:3 (January 1934), pp. 129–138.

Heim, Roger; Francoise Flieder; and Jacqueline Nicot. "Combating the Moulds Which Develop on Cultural Property in Tropical Climates." In *The Conservation of Cultural Property with Special Reference to Tropical Conditions* (Paris: UNESCO, 1968), pp. 41–52. ♦ Includes preventive measures, building location, materials, design, air conditioning, sanitation, remedial measures, disinfection in oven and autoclave, decontamination of storerooms and exhibit rooms, types of mold, microorganisms which attack stone, microorganisms which attack timber.

Honig, Mervin. "The Problem of Fungus Infestation of a Framed Pastel Portrait on Paper," *Bulletin of the American Group—IIC,* 11:2 (April 1971), pp. 129–131.

Minich, A., and M. Gell. "Mould Growth on Painted Surfaces," *Paint Technology,* 17 (1952), pp. 426–429.

U.S. Department of Agriculture. *How to Prevent and Remove Mildew: Home Methods.* Rev. Home and Garden Bulletin no. 68. Washington, D.C.: 1970. 12 pp.

6

Conservation of Library Materials

Museum and historical society libraries frequently have more rare books, more manuscripts, and more old photographs and maps than ordinary libraries. The result is more problems of conservation and preservation, and in far too many cases there have been no significant attempts to solve those problems.

It will be difficult to find conservators to deal with book conservation, as has been pointed out by Paul N. Banks, Conservator at the Newberry Library, in a recently released statement on "Professional Training in Library and Archives Conservation." The fact is that book conservation is in a transitional phase and there are no specialized training programs.

An optimistic note can be offered: there are a large number of procedures that can be performed by staff members or volunteers who have acquired, at workshops or seminars or through special courses, the necessary background for understanding what to do and what not to do. These paraprofessionals can profit from a careful review of the references cited in this chapter.

The situation in document conservation is somewhat more encouraging since the regular conservation programs do provide training in the techniques of paper conservation. In addition significant progress is being made in the techniques of photographic conservation as museums and historical societies become aware of the value and importance of their photographic resources. Conservation of sound recordings is still in its infancy as is evidenced by the paucity of references on this subject.

General Reference

Banks, Paul N. *Professional Training in Library and Archives Conservation*. Chicago: The Newberry Library, 1975. 4 pp.

Cunha, George M. "National Trends in Cooperative Approaches to Conservation," Pennsylvania Library Association *Bulletin*, 28:6 (November 1973), pp. 226–231.

Cunha, George M. "A Regional Restoration Center for New England," *Bulletin of the American Institute for Conservation of Historic and Artistic Works,* 13:2 (1973), pp. 6–16. ♦ A description of the New England Document Conservation Center.

Cunha, George M., and Dorothy Grant

Cunha. *Conservation of Library Materials: A Manual and Bibliography on the Care, Repair and Restoration of Library Materials*. 2nd ed. Metuchen, N.J.: Scarecrow Press, 1971–1972. 2 vols. ♦ Vol. I includes chapters on historical background, the nature of library materials, the enemies of library materials, preventive care, repair and restoration and emergency measures. Vol. II is a bibliography on the history of bookbinding, materials, enemies of books, environmental factors in conservation, conservation of leather, paper, parchment, vellum, cloth, exotic materials, film, tapes, discs, repair and restoration of binding, paper, leather, parchment, vellum, maps, manuscripts, prints and drawings, seals, and conservation in the tropics.

Deterioration and Preservation of Library

Materials; The Thirty-Fourth Annual Conference of the Graduate Library School, August 4–6, 1969. Edited by Howard W. Winger and Richard D. Smith. Chicago: University of Chicago Press, 1970. 200 pp., bibliog., illus. ♦ Includes the nature of paper, environmental factors, preservation of photographic images, binding practice.

Doms, Keith. "Preservation of Library Materials," Pennsylvania Library Association *Bulletin,* 28:6 (November 1973), entire issue.

Florence, Italy. Biblioteca Nazionale Centrale. *The Restoration System of the Biblioteca Nazionale Centrale di Firenze.* 2nd ed. Florence: The Biblioteca, 1970. 29 pp.

Friedman, Hannah, and Wayne Eley. *Conservation of Library Materials: A Suggested Reading List.* New York: New York Public Library, 1973. 4 pp.

Hasznos, Lola. "Modern Methods for the Protection of Archival and Library Material," *UNESCO Bulletin for Libraries,* 24:6 (November–December 1970), pp. 302–304.

Henderson, James W., and Robert C. Krupp. "The Librarian as Conservator," *The Library Quarterly,* 40:1 (January 1970), pp. 176–191.

Horton, Carolyn. *Cleaning and Preserving Bindings and Related Materials.* 2nd ed., rev. Chicago: Library Technology Project, American Library Association, 1969. 87 pp., illus., bibliog., paperback. ♦ Includes information on reconditioning a library, sorting books and identifying problems and treatment of worn and damaged books; list of supplies and equipment, sources of supply and a glossary. This helpful and clearly written book provides much practical advice to the novice.

Horton, Carolyn. "Saving the Libraries of Florence," *Wilson Library Bulletin,* 41:10 (June 1967), pp. 1035–1043.

Keck, Sheldon. *Emergency Care of Museum Artifacts and Library Materials Affected by the Flood.* Unpublished, on deposit at the New York State Historical Association Library, Cooperstown, New York, 1972. 3 pp., mimeo.

Kimberly, Arthur E., and J.F.G. Hicks, Jr. *A Survey of Storage Conditions in Libraries Relative to the Preservation of Records.* U.S. Bureau of Standards Miscellaneous Publication no. 128. Washington, D.C.: U.S. Government Printing Office, 1931. 8 pp., tables.

Moscow. Publichnaia Biblioteka. *Collection of Materials on the Preservation of Library Resources, Nos. 2 and 3.* Jerusalem: Israel Program for Scientific Translation, 1964. 258 pp., charts, graphs. ♦ No. 2 includes prevention of ageing in books and newspapers; measures to counteract mold, fungi and insects. No. 3 includes studies in the ageing of paper; reinforcement of papers and documents; softening leather; removing dyestuffs from paper; an antiseptic that prevents mold growth in glued paper; shortwave ultraviolet irradiation that disinfects the atmosphere; insect and mold fungi control. Available from the National Technical Information Service, 5285 Port Royal Road, Springfield, Virginia 22151.

New York (City). Public Library. Research Libraries. *Memorandum on Conservation of the Collections.* By James W. Henderson. New York: The New York Public Library, 1970. 28 pp.

New York (State) Library Extension Division. *Your Book Collection: Its Care.* Albany, N.Y.: 1957. 32 pp., illus. ♦ Discusses the physical appearance and appeal of a collection as a whole.

Rineer, A. Hunter, Jr. "Conservation: The Job That Needs to be Done," Pennsylvania Library Association *Bulletin,* 28:6 (November 1973), pp. 221–225.

Schefrin, R.A. "Barriers to and Barriers of Library Security," *Wilson Library Bulletin,* 45:9 (May 1971), pp. 870–878.

Scriven, Margaret. "Preservation and Restoration of Library Materials," *Special Libraries,* 47 (December 1956), pp. 439–448. ♦ Includes list of materials used in preservation and restoration.

Seminar on the Application of Chemical and Physical Methods to the Conservation of Library and Archival Material, Topsfield, Mass., 1971. *Library and Archives Conservation. The Boston Atheneum's 1971 Seminar.* Edited by George M. Cunha and Norman P. Tucker. Boston: Library of the Boston Atheneum, 1972. 255 pp., illus., bibliog. references. ♦ Includes information on materials, fungus deterioration, insect damage, control of light, acid deterioration, environmental control and storage.

Smith, Richard D. "Guidelines for Preservation," *Special Libraries,* 59:8 (May–June

1968), pp. 346–352. ◆ Recommends a written preservation policy for each library.

Smith, Richard D. "New Approaches to Preservation," *Library Quarterly*, 40:1 (January 1970), pp. 139–171.

Tauber, Maurice F. "Conservation Comes of Age," *Library Trends*, 4:3 (January 1956), pp. 215–222.

Tauber, Maurice F., ed. "Conservation of Library Materials," *Library Trends*, 4:3 (January 1956), entire issue.

Waters, Peter. *Procedures for Salvage of Water-Damaged Library Materials*. Washington, D.C.: Library of Congress, 1975. 30 pp., sources of supplies, list of experts.

Wessel, Carl J. "Environmental Factors Affecting the Permanence of Library Materials," *Library Quarterly*, 40:1 (January 1970), pp. 39–84.

Williams, Edwin F. "Deterioration of Library Collections Today," *Library Quarterly*, 40:1 (January 1970), pp. 3–17.

Wilson, William K. "Record Papers and Their Preservation," *Chemistry*, 43:3 (March 1970), pp. 8–12.

Wilson, William K., and James L. Gear. *Care of Books, Documents, Prints and Films*. National Bureau of Standards Consumer Information Series 5. Washington, D.C.: U.S. Government Printing Office, 1971. 16 pp., illus., bibliog.

NOTES AND PERIODICALS

Barrow (W.J.) Laboratory. W.J. Barrow Restoration Shop, Inc., State Library Building, Eleventh and Capitol Street, Richmond, Virginia 23219. The W.J. Barrow Laboratory conducts investigations related to the preservation of library materials. The W.J. Barrow Restoration Shop renders restoration services on a commercial basis.

Library Journal. 1876, semimonthly (September to June), monthly (July–August), subscription. R.R. Bowker Company, 1180 Avenue of the Americas, New York, New York 10036. ◆ Available in microfilm.

Library of Congress Preservation Office. Contact Assistant Director for Preservation, Administrative Department, Library of Congress, Washington, D.C. 20540. The Preservation Office of the Library of Congress was established to provide reference and consultation services in the fields of preservation, restoration, and protection of library materials. It will answer, without charge, brief technical inquiries on matters relating to preservation, restoration, protection and physical custody of materials.

The research program of the Preservation Office investigates problems of paper conservation and such related fields as adhesives, bookbindings, microfilms, magnetic tape, and motion picture film.

The Preservation Office is publishing a series of leaflets devoted to the conservation of books, manuscripts, prints and drawings, and other library and archival materials. For the most part, they are intended for the individual, the librarian, or the archivist with a need for basic information on the preservation of relatively small collections but with limited background and experience in the conservation of books and documents. The first three leaflets are: *Selected References in the Literature of Conservation; Environmental Protection of Books and Related Materials; Preserving Leather Bookbindings*. These and any future leaflets are available free of charge from the Preservation Office at the above address.

The Library Quarterly: A Journal of Investigation and Discussion in the Field of Library Science. 1931, quarterly, subscription. University of Chicago Press, 5801 Ellis Avenue, Chicago, Illinois 60636.

Library Trends. 1952, quarterly, subscription. University of Illinois Press, Subscription Department, Urbana, Illinois 61801.

New England Document Conservation Center. Merrimack Valley Textile Museum, Post Office Box 446, North Andover, Massachusetts 01845. The New England Document Conservation Center was established to make available to public libraries, state and local archival agencies, and participating nonprofit cultural, historical and educational institutions in New England, conservation services on a cooperative basis. The purpose of the Center is to administer and supervise a workshop with the necessary facilities and staff to restore, preserve and maintain the physical condition of books, prints, maps, broadsides, manuscripts, and similar documentary materials of historic, archival or cultural interest.

The Center is authorized by the terms of a library agreement subscribed to by the administration of the New England Interstate Library Compact and approved by the attorneys general of each state.

Paper Conservation News. 1973, six issues per year, subscription. H. Wayne Eley and Associates, 15 Broadway, New Haven, Connecticut 06511. ♦ A newsletter on the subject of paper conservation as applied to all types of paper—books, manuscripts, documents, works of art on paper, etc.

Regional Historical Resource Depositories System. Texas Library and Historical Commission, 1201 Brazos, Box 12927, Capitol Station, Austin, Texas 78711. The Regional Historical Resource Depositories System was designed to provide physical preservation and security copies of records; to professionally arrange and catalog them; and to provide additional storage for historical records that have outgrown local facilities.

Restaurator: International Journal for Preservation of Library and Archival Material. 1969, three issues per year, subscription. Restaurator Press, Postbox 96, DK 1004, Copenhagen K, Denmark. ♦ Articles based on research and experience of laboratories, libraries and archives. Text in English, French, German and Russian.

Society of Archivists Journal. 1955, semi-annual, membership. Society of Archivists, Guildhall Library, Basinghall Street, London, EC2, England.

Wilson Library Bulletin. 1914, monthly (September–June), subscription. H.W. Wilson Company, 950 University Avenue, Bronx, New York 10452. ♦ Available in microform.

Materials

American Paper and Pulp Association. The Dictionary of Paper, Including Pulp, Paperboard, Paper Properties and Related Papermaking Terms. 3rd ed. New York: American Paper and Pulp Association, 1965. 500 pp., bibliog.

Arad, A. "A Simple Measurement of Torsional Rigidity of Paper," Restaurator, 1:2 (1969), pp. 69–77.

Arad, A. "Tear-Resistance Instrument," Restaurator, 1:3 (1970), pp. 165–176.

Armitage, F.K. An Atlas of the Commoner Paper Making Fibres; An Introduction to Paper Microscopy. London: Guildhall Publishing Co., 1957. 172 pp., illus. ♦ Includes microphotographs of fibers.

Avedon, Don M. "Microfilm Permanence and Archival Quality," Special Libraries, 63:12 (December 1972), pp. 586–588.

Baer, Norbert S.; N. Indictor; and A. Joel. "An Evaluation of Glues for Use in Paper Construction." In Conservation of Paintings and the Graphic Arts (London: International Institute for Conservation of Historic and Artistic Works, 1972), pp. 601–612.

Barrow, William James. The Manufacture and Testing of Durable Book Papers. Edited by Randolph W. Church. Virginia State Library Publications no. 13. Richmond: Virginia State Library, 1960. 63 pp., diagrams, tables, bibliog.

Barrow (W.J.) Research Laboratory. Permanence/Durability of the Book: A Two-Year Research Program. Publication No. 1. Richmond, Va.: W.J. Barrow Research Laboratory, 1963. 46 pp., photos, tables, graphs, bibliog., paperback.

Barrow (W.J.) Research Laboratory. Permanence/Durability of the Book—II: Test Data of Naturally Aged Papers. Publication No. 2. Richmond, Va.: W.J. Barrow Research Laboratory, 1964. 79 pp., photos, tables, graphs, bibliog., paperback.

Barrow (W.J.), Research Laboratory. Permanence/Durability of the Book—III: Spray Deacidification. Publication No. 3. Richmond, Va.: W.J. Barrow Research Laboratory, 1964. 62 pp., photos, tables, graphs, bibliog., paperback.

Barrow (W.J.) Research Laboratory. Permanence/Durability of the Book—IV: Polyvinyl Acetate (PVA) Adhesives for Use in Library Bookbinding. Publication No. 4 Richmond, Va.: W.J. Barrow Research Laboratory, 1965. 66 pp., photos, tables, appendix, paperback.

Barrow (W.J.) Research Laboratory. Permanence/Durability of the Book—V: Strength and Other Characteristics of Book Papers, 1800–1899. Publication No. 5. Richmond, Va.: W.J. Barrow Research Laboratory, 1967. 116 pp., tables, graphs, appendices, bibliog., paperback.

Barrow (W.J.) Research Laboratory, Inc. *Permanence/Durability of the Book—VI: Spot Testing for Unstable Modern Book and Record Papers.* Publication No. 6. Richmond, Va.: W.J. Barrow Laboratory, 1969. 28 pp., color chart, tables, bibliog., paperback.

Browning, B.L. *Analysis of Paper.* New York: Marcel Dekker, Inc., 1969. 342 pp., illus., bibliog.

Browning, B.L. "The Nature of Paper," *Library Quarterly,* 40:1 (January 1970), pp. 18–38.

Byrne, Jerry, and Jack Weiner. *Permanence.* Appleton, Wisc.: Institute of Paper Chemistry, 1964. 115 pp. ♦ A bibliography on permanence of paper.

Hunter, Dard. *Papermaking, the History and Technique of an Ancient Craft.* 2nd ed., rev. and enl. New York: Alfred A. Knopf, 1947. 611 pp., illus., map, diagrams, bibliog.

Institute of Paper Chemistry. *Aspects of the Taiwanian Handmade Paper Industry.* Film, 21 minutes, 16 mm., color, sound (1966). ♦ Available for rent or purchase from the Institute of Paper Chemistry, P.O. Box 1048, Appleton, Wisconsin 54911.

Joel, A.; N. Indictor; J.F. Hanlan; and N.S. Baer. "The Measurement and Significance of pH in Paper Conservation," *Bulletin of the American Group—IIC,* 12:2 (April 1972), pp. 119–125.

Leisinger, Albert H. *Microphotography for Archives.* Washington, D.C.: International Council on Archives, 1968. 52 pp., bibliog. ♦ Defines types of microforms and gives their advantages and disadvantages. It also discusses microfilm equipment, operations, storage, and maintenance of various formats.

Stout, George L., and Minna H. Horwitz. "Experiments with Adhesives for Paper," *Technical Studies in the Field of the Fine Arts,* III:1 (July 1934), pp. 38–46.

Veaner, Allen B. *The Evaluation of Micropublications: A Handbook for Librarians.* Chicago: Library Technology Program, American Library Association, 1971. 59 pp., illus., bibliog. ♦ Evaluates technical aspects of micropublications, including archival permanence.

Veitch, Fletcher Pearre. *Paper-Making Materials and Their Conservation.* U.S. Department of Agriculture, Bureau of Chemistry Circular 41. Washington, D.C.: U.S. Government Printing Office, 1911. 20 pp.

Wilson, William K. "Reflections on the Stability of Paper," *Restaurator,* 1:2 (1969), pp. 79–86.

Conservation Techniques

Books and Manuscripts

Academy of Sciences of the U.S.S.R. Laboratory for the Conservation and Restoration of Books. *New Methods for the Restoration and Preservation of Documents and Books.* Jerusalem: Israel Program for Scientific Translations, 1964. 124 pp., illus., bibliog. ♦ Includes the use of high frequency electromagnetic fields as a means of disinfecting books; the coating of paper with thermoplastic film; the improvement of faded texts by photographic and radiographic methods. Available from the National Technical Information Service, 5285 Port Royal Road, Springfield, Virginia 22151.

Academy of Sciences of the U.S.S.R. Laboratory for the Conservation and Restoration of Books. *Preservation of Documents and Papers.* Jerusalem: Israel Program for Scientific Translations, 1964. 134 pp., charts, graphs, tables, bibliog., paperback. ♦ Includes investigations on the ageing of papers; preservation of paper documents; new materials and methods in book restoration; new methods of examination of documents; stain removal; conditions of storage of documents in archives. Available from the National Technical Information Service, 5285 Port Royal Road, Springfield, Virginia 22151.

Adams, Randolph G. "Librarians as Enemies of Books," *The Library Quarterly,* 7:3 (July 1937), pp. 317–331. ♦ Also published in Marshall, John D., et al., eds. *Books, Libraries, Librarians.* Hamden, Conn.: Shoestring Press, 1955.

Amber, George H. *Water Damaged Files, Papers and Records: What To Do About Them.* Royal Oak, Mich.: Document Reclamation Service, Inc., 1963. 26 pp., illus., bibliog ♦ Suggestions for the handling of books in a large scale emergency. Available from Document Reclamation Service, Inc., Box 261, Royal Oak, Michigan 48068.

American Library Association. Library

Technology Program. *Development of Performance Standards for Library Binding, Phase I.* Report of the Survey Team, April 1961. Chicago: Library Technology Project, American Library Association, 1961. 62 pp.

American Library Association. Library Technology Program. *Development of Performance Standards for Binding Used in Libraries, Phase II.* Report on a Study Conducted by the Library Technology Project. Chicago: Library Technology Project, American Library Association, 1966. 53 pp., illus., paperback.

Archer, H. Richard, ed. *Rare Book Collections; Some Theoretical and Practical Suggestions for Use by Librarians and Students.* Chicago: American Library Association, 1965. 128 pp., bibliog., paperback. ◆ Suggestions for use by librarians and students on the nature and importance of rare books; the rare book library and the public; housing and equipment; care; maintenance and storage.

Association of Research Libraries. Committee on the Preservation of Research Library Materials. *The Preservation of Deteriorating Books: An Examination of the Problem with Recommendations for a Solution; Report.* Washington, D.C.: The Association, 1964. 33 pp., tables, bibliog. footnotes. ◆ See also Williams, Gordon R. "The Preservation of Deteriorating Books, Parts I & II," *Library Journal,* 91:1&2 (January 1966), pp. 51–56; 189–194.

Banister, Manly. *Pictorial Manual of Bookbinding.* New York: The Ronald Press Co., 1958. 40 pp., illus.

Banks, Paul N. "Lamination,'" *Paper Conservation News,* 1:1 (May 1973), pp. 1–3.

Banks, Paul N. "Paper Cleaning," *Restaurator,* 1:1 (1969), pp. 52–66. ◆ Discusses dry, wet and solvent methods of cleaning paper.

Banks, Paul N. *Treating Leather Bookbinding.* Rev. ed. Chicago: Newberry Library, 1967. 4 pp., photocopy.

Banks, Paul N. "The Treatment of an 1855 British Paper Specimen Book," *Bulletin of the American Group—IIC,* 12:2 (April 1972), pp. 88–95.

Barrow, William J. *The Barrow Method of Restoring Deteriorated Documents,* Rev. ed. Richmond, Va.: W.J. Barrow Restoration Shop,

Inc., 1970. 20 pp., bibliog., appendix, paperback.

Barrow, William J. "Deacidification and Lamination of Deteriorated Documents, 1938–1963," *The American Archivist,* 28:2 (April 1965), pp. 285–290.

Barrow, William J. *Manuscripts and Documents: Their Deterioration and Restoration.* 2nd ed. Charlottesville, Va.: University Press of Virginia, 1972. 84 pp., illus., bibliog.

Barrow, William J. *Procedures and Equipment Used in the Barrow Method of Restoring Manuscripts and Documents.* Richmond, Va.: The Author, 1952. 14 pp., bibliog.

Basile, Corrado. "A Method of Making Papyrus and Fixing and Preserving It by Means of a Chemical Treatment." In *Conservation of Paintings and the Graphic Arts* (London: International Institute for Conservation of Historic and Artistic Works, 1972), pp. 901–906.

Baughman, Roland. "Conservation of Old and Rare Books," *Library Trends,* 4:3 (January 1956), pp. 239–247.

Baynes-Cope, A.D. "The Non-Aqueous Deacidification of Documents," *Restaurator,* 1:1 (1969), pp. 2–9.

Belaya, I.K. "Methods of Strengthening the Damaged Leather of Old Bindings," *Restaurator,* 1:2 (1969), pp. 93–104.

Belaya, I.K. "Selecting and Testing Adhesives for the Restoration of Skin-Bindings and Parchments," *Restaurator,* 1:4 (1970), pp. 221–231.

Belaya, I.K. "Softening and Restoration of Parchment in Manuscripts and Bookbindings," *Restaurator,* 1:1 (1969), pp. 20–51.

Blades, William. *The Enemies of Books.* 3rd ed., rev. and enl. New York: A.C. Armstrong & Son, 1888. 165 pp., illus. ◆ Discusses fire, water, gas and heat, dust and neglect, bookworms, other vermin, incompetent bookbinders and careless collectors. Of historical interest.

Boy Scouts of America. *Bookbinding.* New Brunswick, N.J.: Boy Scouts of America, 1969. 24 pp., illus., bibliog., paperback.

Cinemagroup Productions. *Fritz and Trudi Eberhardt, Bookbinders.* Film, 27 minutes, 16 mm., color, optical sound track (1971). ◆ Available for rent or purchase from Cinemagroup Productions, 32 West Queen Lane, Philadelphia, Pennsylvania 19144.

Clarkson, Christopher, and the Library of Congress. *Rebinding in Limp Vellum.* Film, 80 minutes, 16 mm., color, sound, free rental (1972). ♦ May be used for television with proper credit to both the producer and the institution.

Clough, Eric A. *Bookbinding for Librarians.* London: Association of Assistant Librarians, 1957. 204 pp., illus., bibliog.

Cockerell, Douglas. *Bookbinding, and the Care of Books; A Textbook for Bookbinders and Librarians.* 5th ed., rev. and reprinted. New York: Pitman Publishing Co., 1962. 345 pp., illus.

Cockerell, Douglas. *Some Notes on Bookbinding.* London: Oxford University Press, 1929. 105 pp., illus. ♦ Discusses the deterioration of the quality of materials used in bindings and gives historical and sociological reasons for its occurrence.

Cockerell, Sydney M. *The Repairing of Books.* 2nd ed. London: Sheppard Press, 1960. 110 pp., illus.

Corderoy, John. *Bookbinding for Beginners.* New York: Watson-Guptill, 1967. 104 pp., illus., tables, diagrams, bibliog.

Crowley, Alfred S. "Repair and Conservation of Palm-Leaf Manuscripts," *Restaurator,* 1:2 (1969), pp. 105–114.

Dadic, Vera, and Tatjana Ribkin. "Techniques of Delaminating Polyethylene Laminates," *Restaurator,* 1:3 (1970), pp. 141–148.

Diehl, Edith. *Bookbinding: Its Background and Technique.* Port Washington, N.Y.: Kennikat Press, c 1946, 1965. 2 vols., illus., glossary, bibliog.

DuPuis, R.N.; J.E. Kusterer, Jr.; and R.C. Sproull. "Evaluation of Langwell's Vapor Phase Deacidification Process," *Restaurator,* 1:3 (1970), pp. 149–164.

Ede, J.R., and W.H. Langwell. "Sulphur Dioxide and Vapour Phase Deacidification." In *Contributions to the London Conference on Museum Climatology* (London: International Institute for Conservation of Historic and Artistic Works, 1968), pp. 37–40.

Eley, Wayne. "Framing Paper Artifacts," *Paper Conservation News,* 1:2 (July 1973), pp. 1–4.

Feller, Robert L. "Thermochemically Activated Oxidation: Mother Nature's Book Burning," Pennsylvania Library Association *Bulletin,* 28:6 (November 1973), pp. 232–242.

French, Hannah Dustin. "Early American Bookbinding By Hand." In *Bookbinding in America* (New York: R.R. Bowker, 1967), pp. 3–127. ♦ Includes appendices on American binders and bindings.

Gallo, Fausta. "Biological Agents Which Damage Paper Materials in Libraries and Archives." In *Recent Advances in Conservation* (London: Butterworths, 1963), pp. 55–61.

Gear, James L. "Lamination After 30 Years: Record and Prospect," *The American Archivist,* 28:2 (April 1965), pp. 293–297.

Gear, James L. "The Repair of Documents— American Beginnings," *The American Archivist,* 26:4 (October 1963), pp. 469–475.

Grant, Julius. *Books and Documents: Dating, Permanence and Preservation.* London: Grafton & Co., 1937. 218 pp., illus., references. ♦ Gives a history of bookmaking and paper.

Grimm, Francis W. *A Primer to Bookbinding.* Boston: Houghton Mifflin Co., 1939. 66 pp., illus., plates, diagrams.

Grove, Lee E. "Care of Paper," *Museum News,* 42:2 (October 1963), pp. 15–20.

Harlow, Neal R. "Physical Housing and Equipment." In *Rare Book Collections* (Chicago: American Library Association, 1970), pp. 86–91.

Hasznos, Lola. "Manual and Mechanical Restoration of Paper Manuscripts." In *Conservation of Painting and the Graphic Arts* (London: International Institute for Conservation of Historic and Artistic Works, 1972), pp. 925–933.

Hawken, William R. *Photocopying From Bound Volumes: A Study of Machines, Methods and Materials.* Chicago: Library Technology Project, American Library Association, 1962. 208 pp., illus.

Hey, Margaret. "The Use of the Scanning Electron Microscope in Document Restoration Problems," *Restaurator,* 1:4 (1970), pp. 233–244.

Hobson, A.R.A. *The Literature of Bookbinding.* London: Cambridge University Press for National Book League, 1954. 15 pp.

Horton, Carolyn. *Conservation of Rare Books, Mss., and Related Materials.* Cooperstown, N.Y.: New York State Historical Association Seminars on American Culture, 1963. 9 pp., illus., bibliog., mimeo.

Horton, Carolyn. *Report and Recommendations on the Rescue of the Water-Damaged Books and Prints at the Corning Glass Center, Corning, New York, June, 1972.* Unpublished, on deposit at the New York State Historical Association Library, Cooperstown, New York, 1972. 4 pp., supplies notes, mimeo. ♦ Report prepared for the Corning Glass Center after flood damage to collection.

Hummel, Ray O., and W.J. Barrow. "Lamination and Other Methods of Preservation," *Library Trends,* 4:3 (January 1956), pp. 259–268.

Jennett, Sean. *The Making of Books.* 4th ed., rev. New York: Frederick E. Praeger, 1967. 512 pp., illus., bibliog.

Kane, Lucile M. *A Guide to the Care and Administration of Manuscripts.* 2nd ed. Nashville, Tenn.: American Association for State and Local History, 1966. 74 pp., illus., bibliog., paperback. ♦ Provides basic information on the care of historical manuscripts. Includes chapters on establishing controls, organizing and sorting collections, evaluation, preservation and cataloguing.

Kathpalia, Yash Pal. *Conservation and Restoration of Archive Materials.* Paris: UNESCO, 1973. 231 pp., illus., bibliog., paperback. ♦ Examines specific problems of conservation and restoration of archive materials in regions with unfavorable climatic conditions. Contents include constituent materials of documents; deterioration; repair; preservation of microfilms and sound recordings; restoration of documents; cleaning, washing and flattening; deacidification; workrooms and equipment; physical and chemical tests; formulae and specifications for ink; pastes.

Kathpalia, Yash Pal. "Hand-Lamination with Cellulose Acetate," *The American Archivist,* 21:3 (July 1958), pp. 271–276.

Kimberly, Arthur, and B.W. Scribner. *Summary Report of National Bureau of Standards Research on Preservation of Records.* National Bureau of Standards Miscellaneous Publications M154. Washington, D.C.: U.S. Government Printing Office, 1937. 28 pp., tables, diagrams.

Klinefelter, Lee M. *Bookbinding Made Easy.* Rev. ed. Milwaukee, Wisc.: The Bruce Publishing Co., 1960. 86 pp., illus.

Knightbridge, A.A.H. "Document Repair: A Bibliography," *Society of Archivists Journal,* 4:2 (October 1970), pp. 137–140.

Lakeside Press. Chicago. *A Rod for the Back of the Binder: Some Considerations of Book Binding with Reference to the Ideals of the Lakeside Press.* Chicago: R.R. Donnelley & Sons Company, 1929. 31 pp., illus.

Langwell, William H. *The Conservation of Books and Documents.* London: Pitman Publishing Co., 1957. 114 pp.

Lee, H.N. "Established Methods for Examination of Paper," *Technical Studies in the Field of the Fine Arts,* IV:1 (July 1935), pp. 3–14.

Lee, H.N. "Improved Methods for the Examination of Paper," *Technical Studies in the Field of the Fine Arts,* IV:2 (October 1935), pp. 93–106.

Lehmann-Haupt, Hellmut. "On the Rebinding of Old Books." In *Bookbinding in America* (New York: R.R. Bowker Company, 1967), pp. 189–283L. ♦ Supplement by the author added in the reprinted edition gives information on recent publication in the fields of bookbinding in general and conservation in particular.

Lehmann-Haupt, Hellmut, ed. *Bookbinding in America: Three Essays.* 1941. Reprint. Supplements by the authors. New York: R.R. Bowker Co., 1967. 293 pp., illus., bibliog. references.

Lewis, Arthur W. *Basic Bookbinding.* New York: Dover Publications, 1957. 144 pp., illus.

Library Binding Institute. *Library Binding Institute Standard for Library Binding.* 4th ed. Boston: Library Binding Institute, 1963. 14 pp. ♦ Library Binding Institute, 160 State Street, Boston, Massachusetts 02109.

Lovett, Robert W. "Old-Time New England Primer of Preservation: P is for Paper." *Old-Time New England,* LIII:4 (April–June 1963), pp. 110–113. ♦ Discusses what to preserve and how to preserve it—family or business records and private papers. Suggests methods of preservation and restoration for the layman.

Lydenberg, Harry Miller, and John Archer. *The Care and Repair of Books.* 4th ed., rev. by John Alden. New York: R.R. Bowker Co., 1960. 122 pp.

McCarthy, Paul. "Vapor Phase Deacidification: A New Preservation Method," *The American Archivist,* 32:4 (October 1969), pp. 333–342.

Marconi, Bohdan. "Some Tests on the Use of Wax for Fixing Flaking Paint on Illuminated Parchment," *Studies in Conservation,* 7:1 (February 1962), pp. 17–21.

Metcalf, Keyes D. "The Design of Book Stacks and the Preservation of Books," *Restaurator,* 1:2 (1969), pp. 115–125.

Middleton, Bernard C. *A History of English Craft Bookbinding Technique.* New York: Hafner Publishing Co., 1963. 307 pp., illus., diagrams, bibliog. footnotes.

Middleton, Bernard C. *The Restoration of Leather Bindings.* Chicago: American Library Association, Library Technology Project, 1972. 201 pp., illus., bibliog., paperback.

Minogue, Adelaide E. "Physical Care, Repair and Protection of Manuscripts," *Library Trends,* 5:3 (January 1957), pp. 344–351.

Minogue, Adelaide E. *The Repair and Preservation of Records.* Bulletin of the National Archives #5. Washington, D.C.: U.S. Government Printing Office, 1943. 56 pp., bibliog., paperback. ♦ Out-of-print but worth consulting; summary of the causes and prevention of decay, and the cleaning and repair of bindings, seals, parchments, and maps.

Mortimer, Edward A. *Library Books: Their Care and Repair; a Handbook for Library Binding Instructors and Librarians.* Auckland, N.Z.: University of Auckland, 1968. 24 pp., illus. ♦ Basic guide for librarians.

National Bureau of Standards. *Protective Display Lighting of Historical Documents: A Report by the National Bureau of Standards to the Library of Congress.* Washington, D.C.: U.S. Government Printing Office, 1953. 8 pp., illus.

Nelson, Clark W., ed. "Specifications for Permanent/Durable Paper for Carbon Copies; Report of the Paper Research Committee of the Society of American Archivists," *The American Archivist,* 35:1 (January 1972), pp. 81–85.

New York. Public Library. *Causes and Prevention of Deterioration in Book Materials.* Compiled by Robert P. Walton. New York: The New York Public Library, 1929. 39 pp.

"P Stands for Permanence," *The Laboratory,* 32:2 (1964), pp. 98–101.

Percival, G.S. *Repairing Books.* Dryad Leaflet no. 150. Leicester, England: The Dryad Press, n.d. 16 pp., illus. ♦ Available from Dryad Handicrafts, Northgates, Leicester, England. In the U.S.: The Craftool Company, 1421 West 240th Street, Harbor City, California 90710.

Phelan, W.H.; N.S. Baer; and N. Indictor. "Adhesives Used in Paper Conservation: A Preliminary Evaluation," *Bulletin of the American Group—IIC,* 11:1 (October 1970), pp. 29–30.

Piez, Gladys. "Archival Containers—A Search for Safer Materials," *The American Archivist,* 27:3 (July 1964), pp. 433–438.

Plumbe, Wilfred J. *The Preservation of Books in Tropical and Subtropical Countries.* Kuala Lumpur: Oxford University Press, 1964. 72 pp., illus., bibliog.

"Practical Problems: Tapes, Adhesives, Protective Wrappers," *Paper Conservation News,* 1:3 (September 1973), pp. 1–4.

"Preservation of Library Materials: A Symposium of the New York Library Association," *Special Libraries,* 59:8 (October 1968), pp. 607–625.

Rhoads, James B. "Alienation and Thievery: Archival Problems," *The American Archivist,* 29:2 (April 1966), pp. 197–208.

Redstone, L.J., and F.W. Steer, eds. *Local Records, Their Preservation and Care.* London: G. Bell and Sons, Ltd., 1953. 246 pp., bibliog.

Rogers, J.S., and C.W. Beebe. *Leather Bookbindings: How to Preserve Them.* U.S.D.A. Leaflet no. 398. Washington, D.C.: U.S. Government Printing Office, 1956. 8 pp., illus. ♦ Supersedes Leaflet no. 69, *Preservation of Leather Bookbindings.*

Rogers, Joseph W. "The Rise of American Edition Binding." In *Bookbinding in America* (New York: R.R. Bowker Co., 1967), pp. 131–185b. ◆ Supplement by the author added in the reprinted edition gives information on recent publications on nineteenth century American edition binding.

Sajor, Ladd Z. "Preservation Microfilming—Why, What, When, Who, How," *Special Libraries,* 63:4 (April 1972), pp. 195–201.

Santen, Vernon, and Howard Crocker. "Historical Society Records: Guidelines for a Protection Program," *History News,* 27:9 (September 1972), Technical Leaflet no. 18 (new series).

Santucci, Ludovico. "The Application of Chemical and Physical Methods to Conservation of Archival Materials." In *Recent Advances in Conservation* (London: Butterworths, 1963), pp. 39–47. ◆ Discusses early attempts at preservation, application of modern science, and the present situation and prospects.

Santucci, Ludovico. "Degradation of Paper Treated with Oxidants Effect of Lamination on the Aging of Paper." In *Problems of Conservation in Museums* (Paris: Editions Eyrolles, 1969), pp. 187–207.

Schick, Frank L. "Trends in Publications Affecting Binding and Conservation," *Library Trends,* 4:3 (January 1956), pp. 222–238.

Scribner, Bourdon W. *Preservation of Newspaper Records.* Washington, D.C.: U.S. Government Printing Office, 1934. 10 pp., tables.

Smith, Richard D. "Paper Deacidification: A Preliminary Report," *The Library Quarterly,* 36:4 (October 1966), pp. 273–292.

Smith, Richard D. "Paper Impermanence as a Consequence of pH and Storage Conditions," *The Library Quarterly,* 39:2 (April 1969), pp. 153–192.

Spawn, William. "After the Water Comes," Pennsylvania Library Association *Bulletin,* 28:6 (November 1973), pp. 242–251.

Storm, Colton. "Care, Maintenance, and Restoration." In *Rare Book Collections* (Chicago: American Library Association, 1970), pp. 74–85.

Tauber, Maurice F., ed. *Library Binding Manual: A Handbook of Useful Procedures for the Maintenance of Library Volumes.* Boston: Library Binding Institute, 1972. 185 pp., illus., glossary, appendices, index.

Tribolet, Harold W. "Binding Practice as Related to Books," *The Library Quarterly,* 40:1 (January 1970), pp. 128–136.

Tribolet, Harold W. "Rare Book and Paper Repair Techniques," rev. ed., *History News,* 25:3 (March 1970), Technical Leaflet no. 13.

Tribolet, Harold W. "Trends in Preservation," *Library Trends,* 13:2 (October 1964), pp. 208–214.

United States. Federal Fire Council. *Salvaging and Restoring Records Damaged by Fire and Water.* Recommended Practices #2. Washington, D.C.: Federal Fire Council, 1963. 17 pp., illus.

U.S. National Bureau of Standards. *Preservation of the Declaration of Independence and the Constitution of the United States: A Report to the Library of Congress.* Washington, D.C.: U.S. Government Printing Office, 1950. 16 pp., illus.

U.S. National Bureau of Standards. Division of Organic and Fibrous Materials. Paper Section. *Preservation of Documents by Lamination.* Washington, D.C.: 1954–1957. 1 vol., various pagings, illus.

"Vapor Phase Process for Mass Deacidification of Paper and Books Developed," *Paper Conservation News,* 1:4 (November 1973), pp. 1–4.

Walters Art Gallery. *The History of Bookbinding, 525–1950 A.D.* An Exhibition held at the Baltimore Museum of Art, November 12, 1957, to January 12, 1958, organized by the Walters Art Gallery and presented in cooperation with the Baltimore Museum of Art. Baltimore: The Trustees of the Walters Art Gallery, 1957. 275 pp., illus., bibliog.

Wardle, D.B. *Document Repair.* Handbook no. 1. London: Society of Archivists, 1971. 84 pp., photos, appendices, index. ◆ Includes causes for damage, workshop equipment, stock control, record keeping, paper repair, parchment restoration, repair of maps and seals, preparing material for exhibition.

Waters, Peter, and the Royal College of

Art. *The Restoration of Books, Florence 1968.* Film, 40 minutes, 16 mm., color, sound (1968). ◆ Shows types of damage, laboratories in Biblioteca Nazionale Centrale, and some excellent shots of binding techniques. May be used for television with proper credit to both the producer and the institution. Available from the Preservation Office, Library of Congress, Washington, D.C. 20540.

Watson, Aldren. *Hand Bookbinding: A Manual of Instruction.* 1st ed. New York: Reinhold Publishing Corp., 1963. 93 pp., illus.

Weber, Carl J. *Fore-Edge Painting: A Historical Survey of a Curious Art in Book Decoration.* Irvington-on-Hudson, N.Y.: Harvey House, 1966. 223 pp., illus., bibliog.

Weiss, H.B., and Ralph H. Carruthers. *Insect Enemies of Books.* New York: The New York Public Library. 1945. 63 pp., bibliog. ◆ Reprinted from the *Bulletin of the New York Public Library,* September–December, 1936.

Wendelbo, O., and B. Fosse. "Protein Surgery: A Restoring Procedure Applied to Paper," *Restaurator,* 1:4 (1970), pp. 245–248. ◆ Describes the use of enzymes for restoring library and archival materials.

Werner, A.E. "The Conservation of Leather, Wood, Bone, Ivory, and Archival Materials." In *The Conservation of Cultural Property with Special Reference to Tropical Conditions* (Paris: UNESCO, 1968), pp. 265–290. ◆ On leather: mould growth, insect attack, brittleness. On wood: adhesives and consolidants, protective coatings, waterlogged wood, painted wood. On bone and ivory: consolidation in the field, treatment in the laboratory. On archival material: control of insects, mould growth, methods of treatment. Includes bibliography.

Werner, A.E. "The Lamination of Documents." In *Problems of Conservation in Museums* (Paris: Editions Eyrolles, 1969), pp. 209–224. ◆ Discusses heat sealing, dry mounting, solvent lamination; evaluation of various methods; deacidification of paper.

Williams, Gordon R. "The Preservation of Deteriorating Books, Part I: An Examination of the Problem," *Library Journal,* 91:1 (January 1, 1966), pp. 51–56. ◆ See also: *The Preservation of Deteriorating Books: An Examination of the Problem with Recom-*mendations for a Solution (Washington, D.C.: Association of Research Libraries, 1964).

Williams, Gordon R. "The Preservation of Deteriorating Books, Part II: Recommendations for a Solution," *Library Journal,* 91:2 (January 15, 1966), pp. 189–194. ◆ See also: *The Preservation of Deteriorating Books: An Examination of the Problem with Recommendations for a Solution* (Washington, D.C.: Association of Research Libraries, 1964).

Williams, John C. "Chemistry of the Deacidification of Paper," *Bulletin of the American Group—IIC,* 12:1 (1971), pp. 16–31.

Wilson, William K., and B.W. Forshee. *Preservation of Documents by Lamination.* National Bureau of Standards Monograph no. 5. Washington, D.C.: U.S. Department of Commerce, National Bureau of Standards, 1959. 20 pp., illus., bibliog., paperback.

Maps

Brown, Lloyd Arnold. *Notes on the Care and Cataloguing of Old Maps.* 1940. Reprint. Port Washington, N.Y.: Kennikat Press, 1970. 110 pp., illus., facsims., bibliog.

Capps, Marie T. "Preservation and Maintenance of Maps," *Special Libraries,* 63:10 (October 1972), pp. 457–463. ◆ Gives advice on air, heat and moisture, light, vermin, mold and fungi, acid and storage.

Easton, William W. "Repair and Preservation of Map Materials," *Special Libraries,* 61:4 (April 1970), pp. 199–200.

Smith, Richard D. "Maps, Their Deterioration and Preservation," *Special Libraries,* 63:2 (February 1972), pp. 59–68.

U.S. Library of Congress. Map Division. *Maps: Their Care, Repair and Preservation in Libraries.* By Clara Egli LeGear. Washington, D.C.: Library of Congress, 1949. 46 pp., illus., bibliog. ◆ Covers processing, care, repair, preservation and storage of maps. Out-of-print but available in facsimile from Xerox University Microfilms, 300 North Zeeb Road, Ann Arbor, Michigan 48106.

Photographic Materials

American National Standards Institute. *American National Standard Practice for*

43

Storage of Processed Safety Photographic Film Other Than Microfilm. New York: American National Standards Institute, Inc., 1971. 12 pp., bibliog., appendices.

American National Standards Institute. American National Standard Practice for Storage of Processed Silver Gelatin Microfilm. New York: American National Standards Institute, Inc., 1970. 16 pp., bibliog., appendices.

American National Standards Institute. American National Standard Specifications for Photographic Film for Archival Records, Silver Gelatin Type on Cellulose Ester Base. New York: American National Standards Institute, Inc., 1973. 16 pp., bibliog., appendices.

American National Standards Institute. American National Standard Specifications for Photographic Film for Archival Records, Silver Gelatin Type on Polyester Base. New York: American National Standards Institute, 1973. 16 pp., bibliog., appendices.

American Standards Association. American Standard Requirements for Photographic Filing Enclosures for Storing Processed Photographic Films, Plates and Papers. New York: The Association, 1959. 7 pp., illus.

American Standards Association. U.S.A. Standard Practice for Storage of Microfilm. New York: United States of American Standards Institute, 1957. 11 pp., bibliog.

Brown, H.G. "Problems of Storing Film for Archive Purposes," British Kinematography, 20 (May 1952), pp. 150–162.

Calhoun, J.M. "Storage of Nitrate Amateur Still-Camera Film Negatives," Journal of the Biological Photographic Association, 21:3 (August 1953), pp. 1–13.

Crabtree, J.I.; G.T. Eaton; and L.F. Meuhler. "The Removal of Hypo and Silver Salts from Photographic Materials as Affected by the Composition of the Processing Solutions," Journal of the Society of Motion Picture Engineers, 41 (July 1943), pp. 9–68.

Crabtree, J.I., and R.W. Henn. "Scums, Sludges, and Stains: Their Sources, Prevention and Removal," PSA Journal, 14 (April 1948), pp. 201–209.

Decker, Francis W. "The Care of Motion Pic-

ture Film," The American Archivist, 25:3 (July 1962), pp. 357–359.

Deschin, Jacob. "Barbara Morgan: Permanence through Perseverance," 1971 Popular Photography Annual, pp. 6–24; 170–171.

Eastman Kodak Company. B/W Processing for Permanence. Rochester, N.Y.: Eastman Kodak Co., 1973. 8 pp., pamphlet.

Eastman Kodak Company. Handling, Repair, and Storage of Eastman Kodak 16mm Motion Picture Film. Rochester, N.Y.: Eastman Kodak Co., 1971. 8 pp., illus., pamphlet.

Eastman Kodak Company. Prevention and Removal of Fungus on Prints and Films. Rochester, N.Y.: Eastman Kodak Co., 1971. 6 pp., pamphlet.

Eastman Kodak Company. Stains on Negatives and Prints. Rochester, N.Y.: Eastman Kodak Co., 1952. 36 pp., illus. ◆ Out-of-print, new edition in progress.

Eastman Kodak Company. Storage and Care of Kodak Color Films. Rochester, N.Y.: Eastman Kodak Co., 1973. 6 pp., illus., pamphlet.

Eastman Kodak Company. Storage and Care of Kodak Films in Rolls. Rochester, N.Y.: Eastman Kodak Company, 1973. 4 pp.

Eastman Kodak Company. Storage and Preservation of Microfilms. Rochester, N.Y.: Eastman Kodak Co., 1972. 11 p., diagrams, bibliog., pamphlet.

Eastman Kodak Company. Storage and Preservation of Motion Picture Film. Rochester, N.Y.: Eastman Kodak Co., 1957. 79 pp., illus., bibliog.

Eastman Kodak Company. Storage of Microfilms, Sheet Films and Prints (Safety Film Base and Paper Base Materials Only). Rochester, N.Y.: Eastman Kodak Co., 1951. 15 pp., bibliog.

Eaton, George T. "Preservation, Deterioration, Restoration of Photographic Images," Library Quarterly, 40:1 (January 1970), pp. 85–98.

The Encyclopedia of Photography; The Complete Photographer: the Comprehensive Guide and Reference for all Photographers

New York: Greystone Press, 1963–1964. 20 vols., illus., bibliog.

The Focal Encyclopedia of Photography. Rev. desk ed. New York: McGraw-Hill Co., 1969. 1699 pp., illus., bibliog.

Henebry, Agnes. "Preservation of Photographs on Microfilm: An Experiment," *Special Libraries,* 47 (December 1956), pp. 451–454.

Henn, R.W.; J.I. Crabtree; and H.D. Russell. "An Ammonium Hypo Reducer," *PSA Journal,* 17B (November 1951), pp. 110–113.

Henn, R.W., and I.A. Olivares. "Tropical Storage of Processed Negatives," *Photographic Science and Engineering,* 4:4 (July–August 1960), pp. 229–233.

Henn, R.W., and D.C. West. "Microscopic Spots in Processed Microfilm, Their Nature and Prevention," *Photographic Science and Engineering,* 7:5 (October 1963), pp. 253–261.

Leisinger, Albert H. *Microphotography for Archives.* Washington, D.C.: International Council on Archives, 1968. 52 pp., bibliog. ♦ Defines types of microforms and gives their advantages and disadvantages. It also discusses microfilm equipment, operations, storage, and maintenance of various formats.

McCamy, C.S. *Inspection of Processed Photographic Records Films for Aging Blemishes.* Washington, D.C.: U.S. Department of Commerce, National Bureau of Standards, 1964. 11 pp., illus. ♦ Available from the U.S. Government Printing Office.

McCamy, C.S., and C.I. Pope. *Summary of Current Research on Archival Microfilm.* National Bureau of Standards Technical Note no. 261. Washington, D.C.: U.S. Department of Commerce, 1965. 24 pp., bibliog.

"Method of Restoring Daguerreotypes," *Bulletin of the Missouri Historical Society,* XIII:1 (October 1956), pp. 86–87.

Montuori, Theodore. "Lesson Learned from Agnes." Reprinted from *The Journal of Micrographics,* 6:3 (January–February 1973), pp. 133–136. ♦ Describes the damage inflicted upon microfilm records by Hurricane Agnes and how the microfilm was salvaged and reclamated. Precautions for microfilm security are also presented.

National Fire Protection Association. *Standard for Storage and Handling of Cellulose Nitrate Motion Picture Film.* Boston: The Association, 1967. 38 pp. ♦ Available from the National Fire Protection Association, 60 Batterymarch Street, Boston, Massachusetts 02110.

Noll, Daniel F. "The Maintenance of Microfilm Files," *The American Archivist,* 13:2 (April 1950), pp. 129–134.

Orraca, Jose. "The Conservation of Photographic Materials," *Bulletin of the American Institute for Conservation of Historic and Artistic Works,* 13:2 (1973), pp. 32–38.

Orraca, Jose. "The Preservation and Restoration of Glass Plate Negatives," *Image,* 16:2 (June 1973), pp. 8–9.

Ostroff, Eugene. "Conserving and Restoring Photographic Collections," *Museum News,* 52:8 (May 1974), pp. 42–45. ♦ This article is the first in a series of four reports on the conservation, restoration, and storage of photographic collections. Discusses environmental contamination, temperature and humidity.

Ostroff, Eugene. "Conserving and Restoring Photographic Collections, Part 2: The Effects of Residual Chemicals," *Museum News,* 53:1 (September 1974), pp. 40–42.

Ostroff, Eugene. "Conserving and Restoring Photographic Collections, Part 3: Restoration," *Museum News,* 53:3 (November 1974), pp. 42–45.

Ostroff, Eugene. "Conserving and Restoring Photographic Collections, Part 4: Storage," *Museum News,* 53:4 (December 1974), pp. 34–36.

Ostroff, Eugene. "Early Fox Talbot Photographs and Restoration by Neutron Irradiation," *The Journal of Photographic Science,* 13 (1965), pp. 213–227.

Ostroff, Eugene. "Preservation of Photographs," *The Photographic Journal,* 107:10 (October 1967), pp. 309–314.

Ostroff, Eugene. "Talbot's Earliest Extant Print, June 20, 1835, Rediscovered," *Photographic Science and Engineering,* 10:6 (November–December 1966), pp. 350–354.

Scribner, Bourdon W. *Summary Report of Research at the National Bureau of Stand-*

ards on the Stability and Preservation of Records on Photographic Film. Washington, D.C.: U.S. Government Printing Office, 1939. 17 pp., diagrams, references.

United States of America Standards Institute. *American Standard Specification for Safety Photographic Film.* New York: U.S.A. Standards Institute, 1965. 7 pp.

Van Ravenswaay, Charles. "An Improved Method for the Restoration of Daguerreotypes," *Image*, 5:7 (September 1956), pp. 156–160.

Vestal, David. "Are Your Prints Fading Away?" *Popular Photography*, 64:4 (April (1969), pp. 67–69; 106–109.

Wagner, Robert W. "Motion Picture Restoration," *The American Archivist*, 32:2 (April 1969), pp. 125–132.

Wagner, Robert W. "Preservation and Restoration of Photographic Materials Through Nuclear and Ultra-Sonic Methods," *Illinois Libraries*, 53:1 (January 1971), pp. 10–17.

Weinstein, Robert A., and Larry Booth. *Collection, Use, and Care of Historic Photographs.* Nashville, Tenn.: American Association for State and Local History, 1977. 222 pp., photos, appendix, bibliog., index.

White, Minor. "Care and Preservation of the Old Photographs and Negatives," *Image*, 4:8 (November 1955), pp. 59–60. ◆ Discusses removal of mounts, stereographs, daguerreotypes, and restoration.

Wilhelm, Henry. *Preservation of Contemporary Photographic Materials.* Grinnell, Iowa: East Street Gallery, 1977. 370 pp., photos, chemical formulae, supply list, bibliog, paperback. ◆ Authoritative and advanced research into the preservation of color materials and modern photographic papers.

Wilhelm, Henry. *Procedures for Processing and Storing Black and White Photographs for Maximum Possible Permanence.* Rev. ed. Grinnell, Iowa: East Street Gallery, 1970. 45 pp., photos, chemical formulae, supply list, bibliog., paperback. ◆ East Street Gallery, Box 616, 732 State Street, Grinnell, Iowa 50112.

NOTES AND PERIODICALS

American National Standards Institute, 1430 Broadway, New York, New York 10018. Serves as a clearinghouse for nationally coordinated voluntary safety, engineering and industrial standards. Formerly: American Engineering Standards Committee, 1918–1928; American Standards Association, 1928–1965; United States of America Standards Institute, 1965–1969.

British Kinematography, Sound & Television. 1936, monthly, membership. British Kinematography, Sound & Television, 110–112 Victoria House, Vernon Place, London, WC1, England.

Image. Journal of Photography of the George Eastman House. 1952, ten issues per year, membership. George Eastman House Associates, 900 East Avenue, Rochester, New York 14607.

Journal of Photographic Science. 1953, bimonthly, membership. Royal Photographic Society of Great Britain, 14 South Andley Street, London W1Y 5DP, England.

Picturescope. 1953. quarterly, subscription. New York Public Library, Picture Collections (Room 73), Fifth Avenue at 42nd Street, New York, New York 10018. ◆ Includes book reviews and articles on preservation and organization of materials. For the professional librarian and picture researcher.

PSA Journal. 1935, monthly, membership. Photographic Society of America, 4704-F North Paulena Street, Chicago, Illinois 60640.

Sound Recordings

Athey, Skipwith W. *Magnetic Tape Recording.* Washington, D.C.: National Aeronautics and Space Administration, 1966. 326 pp., illus., bibliog. ◆ Distributed by the National Technical Information Service, 5285 Port Royal Road, Springfield, Virginia 22151.

Hall, David. "Phonorecord Preservation, Notes of a Pragmatist," *Special Libraries,* 62:9 (September 1971), pp. 357–262.

Mohrlandt, Victor A. "Tips on Tape Storage." Reprinted from *Broadcast Engineering,* July 1961. 2 pp. ◆ Reprints available from Magnetic Products Division, 3M Company, 2501 Hudson Road, St. Paul, Minnesota 55719.

Pickett, A.G., and M.M. Lemcoe. *Preserva-*

tion and Storage of Sound Recordings: A Study Supported by a Grant from the Rockefeller Foundation. Washington, D.C.: Library of Congress, 1959. 74 pp., illus., diagrams, tables, bibliog. ◆ Available from the U.S. Government Printing Office, Washington, D.C. 20402.

3M Company. Product Communications. Magnetic Products Division. *Magnetic Tape Erasure—How Serious is the Threat.* St. Paul, Minn.: 3M Company, 1972. 5 pp. ◆ Available from Magnetic Products Division, 3M Company, 2501 Hudson Road, St. Paul, Minnesota 55719.

7

Conservation of Paintings

Conservation of paintings is a very specialized aspect of the total conservation effort. It requires specific knowledge, skills and techniques. This chapter is divided into four sections: General Reference; Methods and Materials of Painting; Examination and Analysis; and Techniques of Conservation and Restoration; and is directed primarily to the professional conservator.

Included in the General Reference section are a few handbooks on basic care to familiarize the layman with the problems and practices involved in the care of paintings. The key references are by Caroline Keck entitled *A Handbook on the Care of Paintings* and *How to Take Care of Your Pictures: A Primer of Practical Information.*

The sections on Materials and Methods of Painting and on Examination and Analysis are concerned with how a painting is made, what it is made of and what techniques are used to obtain this information. Art historical and scientific expertise are combined in the analytical and diagnostic process which must, in every instance, precede treatment. The conservator is confronted with such problems as fire damage, water damage, mould growth, cleavage of the paint surface and blistering. The techniques used by conservators to treat paintings include such procedures as cleaning, consolidation, transfer, relining and retouching. These techniques are described in the references in the last section of this chapter. They are highly technical procedures which should be performed only by professional conservators.

General Reference

Agrawal, O.P. *An Introduction to the Preservation of Painting.* Baroda, India: Department of Museology, University of Baroda, 1967. 40 pp., illus., bibliog. ◆ Detailed description of the methods used to preserve paintings from deterioration in the difficult climatic conditions prevailing in India.

American Federation of Arts. "Preserve Your Pictures: A Handbook on the Care and Preservation of Works of Art," American Federation of Arts *Quarterly,* 1:4 (1963), entire issue.

"Basic Care of Paintings," *Canadian Conservation Institute Newsletter,* 1:3 (April 1974), pp. 3–5.

Boustead, William M. "The Conservation of Works of Art in Tropical and Sub-tropical Zones." In *Recent Advances in Conservation* (London: Butterworths, 1963), pp. 73–78.

Bradley, Morton C. *The Treatment of Pictures.* Cambridge, Mass.: Art Technology, 1950. 304 pp., illus., index (incomplete), looseleaf. ◆ Out of print.

Brooklyn Institute of Arts and Sciences, Museum. *Exposition of Painting Conservation: Materials, Methods, Machines.* Brooklyn, N.Y.: The Institute, 1962. diagrams, folio. ◆ Out of print.

"The Care of Old Paintings," *UNESCO Courier,* 18 (January 1965), pp. 14–17.

Coremans, Paul. "The Conservation of Paintings," *Museums Journal,* 61:2 (September 1961), pp. 105–109.

Crawford, B.H. "Just Perceptible Colour Differences in Relation to Level of Illumination," *Studies in Conservation,* 18:4 (November 1973), pp. 159–166.

Feller, Robert L.; Nathan Stolow; and Elizabeth H. Jones. *On Picture Varnishes and Their Solvents.* Rev and enl. ed. Cleveland: Press of Case Western Reserve University, 1971. 251 pp., illus., bibliog., paperback. ◆ Based on the principal papers presented at a Seminar on Resinous Surface Coatings sponsored by the Intermuseum Conservation Association, Oberlin, Ohio.

International Centre for the Study of the Preservation and the Restoration of Cultural Property. *Conservation of Mural Paintings in Different Countries: Report on the General Situation.* Works and Publications no. 2. Rome: Published with the cooperation of the International Council of Museums, 1960. 23 pp. ◆ Text in English and French.

International Film Bureau, Inc. *A Future for the Past.* Film, 20 minutes, 16 mm., black and white, sound, (1954).◆ Sheldon Keck demonstrates examination, hand re-lining, cleaning and compensation of an 18th century portrait. Available from the International Film Bureau, Inc., 332 S. Michigan Ave., Chicago, Illinois 60604.

International Institute for Conservation of Historic and Artistic Works. *Conservation of Paintings and the Graphic Arts.* Preprints of Contributions to the Lisbon Congress, October 9–14, 1972. London: The Institute, 1972. 1006 pp., illus., bibliog. ◆ Includes painting methods and materials; modern media and varnishes; Portuguese painting techniques; Indian paintings; Japanese painting; technology of adhesives; identification of paint media; practical painting restoration.

International Museum Office. *Manual on the Conservation of Paintings.* Paris: The Office, 1940. 296 pp., illus., paperback.

Keck, Caroline K. "Conservation," *History News,* February 1974–1975. ◆ Bimonthly column on conservation.

Keck, Caroline K. *A Handbook on the Care of Paintings.* Rev. ed. Nashville, Tenn.: American Association for State and Local History, 1967. 136 pp., photos, tables, sources of supply, glossary, bibliog., index. ◆ Contains basic information for historical societies on the precau-tions to be taken for the conservation of paintings. Includes descriptions of the physical structure of paintings, the techniques of laboratory examination and treatment performed by conservators and a discussion of conservation priorities and procedures. Intended as practical instruction for curators and custodians not as a manual of conservation techniques.

Keck, Caroline K. *How to Take Care of Your Pictures: A Primer of Practical Information.* New York: Museum of Modern Art and the Brooklyn Museum, c 1954, 1965. 54 pp., illus., paperback. ◆ This handbook is directed toward the layman and includes information on structural composition of a canvas painting; small problems and what to do about them; cleaning a painting yourself; varnishing; familiar misfortunes and how to prevent them; serious troubles and first aid; what happens when a painting is restored.

Keck, Caroline K. "On Conservation: Framing Specifications," *Museum News,* 50:5 (January 1972), pp. 10–11.

Keck, Sheldon. "The Care of Paintings," *New York History,* XLXI:1 (January 1953), pp. 105–120.

Keck, Sheldon, and Caroline K. Keck. *Conservation of Paintings.* New York State Historical Association Seminars on American Culture, 1962. Cooperstown, N.Y.: New York State Historical Association, 1962. 10 pp., bibliog., mimeo.

Kühn, Hermann. "Terminal Dates for Paintings Derived from Pigment Analysis." In *Application of Science in the Examination of Works of Art; Proceedings of the Seminar: June 15–19, 1970* (Boston: Museum of Fine Arts, 1973), pp. 199–205.

Landon, Edward. *Picture Framing: Modern Methods of Making and Finishing Picture Frames.* New York: American Artists Group, Inc., 1945. 146 pp., illus., diagrams.

Lawson, Edward P., ed. "A Panel on Conservation: Painting, Paper and Wood," *Museum News,* 49:5 (January 1971), pp. 27–29.

Museum (Paris). *The Care of Paintings.* UNESCO Publications #778. Paris: UNESCO, 1951. 161 pp., illus. ◆ Issued as a special number of *Museum,* French and English. Includes a detailed analysis of the treatment of ten paintings in the National Gallery, London, and commentary by several European conservators on problems they have faced.

"On Conservation," *Museum News,* November 1971–. Monthly column (September–May) on conservation. ◆ Special conservation topics have been authored by Caroline Keck, Lawrence Majewski and Richard Buck.

Pars, H.H., pseud. *Pictures in Peril.* Translated from the German by Kathrine Talbot. New York: Oxford University Press, 1957. 240 pp., illus. ◆ Traces the history of paintings stolen, mutilated, burnt or badly cared for, and pictures subjected to the ravages and pillages of war. A chapter is devoted to restoration.

Roche, Roger. *Conservation—Necessity and Functions.* Picture Conservation Report no. 3. Ottawa: Public Archives of Canada, 1971. 16 pp., illus.

Stout, George L. *The Care of Pictures.* 1948. Reprint. New York: Dover Publications, Inc., 1974. 125 pp., illus., bibliog., paperback. ◆ A compendium of information on deterioration and remedial care.

Stout, George L. "A Museum Record of the Condition of Paintings," *Technical Studies in the Field of the Fine Arts,* III:4 (April 1935), pp. 200–216.

Taylor, J.M. "Rock Art Studies at the Canadian Conservation Institute," *Canadian Conservation Institute Newsletter,* 1:2 (January 1974), pp. 5–6.

Torraca, Giorgio. "Deterioration Processes of Mural Paintings." In *Application of Science in the Examination of Works of Art; Proceedings of the Seminar: June 15–19, 1970* (Boston: Museum of Fine Arts, 1973), pp. 170–175. ◆ Discusses biological attack, evaporation, condensation, air pollution, surface incrustation, dehydration, rain, sunlight, oxidation, temperature, frost and wind.

Turvey, Helen R. "Filming the Conservation of a Painting," *Museum News,* 45:9 (May 1967), pp. 23–27.

Yale University Art Gallery. *Italian Primitives: The Case History of a Collection and Its Conservation.* New Haven, Conn.: Yale University, 1972. 56 pp., photos, glossary, bibliog. notes, paperback. ◆ A comprehensive exhibition celebrating the centenary of Yale University's acquisition of the Jarves Collection, with emphasis on the history of the collection and the role played by conservation in increasing our understanding of early panel paintings and the changes which time, taste and abuse have inflicted.

Methods and Materials of Painting

Barry, T. Hedley. *Natural Varnish Resins.* London: E. Benn, Ltd., 1932. 294 pp., illus., diagrams. ◆ Background to the history, use and properties of natural resins used in varnishes.

Bazzi, Maria. *The Artist's Methods and Materials.* Translated by Francesca Priuli. London: John Murray, 1960. 228 pp., illus. ◆ Includes surfaces for easel pictures and their preparation, grounds for mural painting, pigments, glues and oils, resins, gums and waxes, varnishes, gilding, pastels, miniatures, watercolors, tempera, oil painting, encaustic, fresco.

Brill, Robert H.; William R. Shields; and J.M. Wampler. "New Directions in Lead Isotope Research." In *Application of Science in the Examination of Works of Art; Proceedings of the Seminar: June 15–19, 1970* (Boston: Museum of Fine Arts, 1973), pp. 73–83.

Butler, Marigene. "An Investigation of Pigments and Technique in the Cezanne Painting, 'Chestnut Trees'," *Bulletin of the American Institute for Conservation of Historic and Artistic Works,* 13:2 (1973), pp. 77–85.

Cennini, Cennino D'Andrea. *The Craftsman's Handbook.* Translated by Daniel V. Thompson, Jr. 1933. Reprint. New York: Dover Publications, 1954. 142 pp., photos, drawings, index, paperback.

Church, Arthur H. *The Chemistry of Paints and Painting.* 4th ed., rev. and enl. London: Seeley and Co., Ltd., 1915. 388 pp., bibliog. notes.

Constable, William G. *The Painter's Workshop.* Boston: Beacon Press, 1963. 148 pp., illus., paperback. ◆ Covers workshop organization and equipment, physical structure of a painting, painting processes (wax, pastel, watercolor, fresco, tempura, oil).

Coomaraswamy, Ananda K. "The Technique and Theory of Indian Painting," *Tech-*

nical Studies in the Field of the Fine Arts, III:2 (October 1934), pp. 59–89.

Doerner, Max. *The Materials of the Artist and Their Use in Painting.* Translated by Eugene Neuhaus. New York: Harcourt, Brace & Co., 1934. 432 pp., illus., bibliog.

Duell, Prentice, and Rutherford J. Gettens. "A Method of Painting in Classical Times," *Technical Studies in the Field of the Fine Arts,* IX:2 (October 1940), pp. 75–104. ◆ Mural Paintings in the Tomba del Letta Funeore in Etruria.

Eastlake, Charles L. *Methods and Materials of Painting of the Great Schools and Masters.* 1847. Reprint. New York: Dover Publications, 1960. 2 vols., paperback. ◆ Unabridged and unaltered republication of the first edition published in 1847 under the title *Materials for a History of Oil Painting.*

Farnsworth, Marie. "Ancient Pigments, Particularly Second Century B.C. Pigments from Corinth." Reprinted from *Journal of Chemical Education,* 28 (February 1951), pp. 72–76.

Federation of Societies for Paint Technology. *Film Formation, Film Properties, and Film Deterioration; A Study by the Research Committee of the Federation of Paint and Varnish Production Clubs.* New York: Interscience Publishers, Inc., 1958. 422 pp., illus., bibliog.

Feller, Robert L. "Felt-Tipped Markers and the Need for Standards of Light Fastness for Artists' Colorants," *Bulletin of the American Group—IIC,* 8:1 (1967), pp. 24–26.

Feller, Robert L. "Identification and Analysis of Resins and Spirit Varnishes." In *Application of Science in the Examination of Works of Art; Proceedings of the Seminar: September 15–18, 1958* (Boston: Museum of Fine Arts, 1959), pp. 51–76.

Feller, Robert L. "New Solvent-Type Varnishes." In *Recent Advances in Conservation* (London: Butterworths, 1963), pp. 171–175.

Feller, Robert L. "A Note on the Exposure of Dammar and Mastic Varnishes to Fluorescent Lamps," *Bulletin of the American Group—IIC,* 4:2 (April 1964), pp. 12–14.

Feller, Robert L. "Polymer Emulsions," *Bulletin of the American Group—IIC,* 6:2 (May 1966), pp. 24–28.

Feller, Robert L. "Problems in the Investigation of Picture Varnishes." In *Conservation of Paintings and the Graphic Arts* (London: International Institute for Conservation of Historic and Artistic Works, 1972), pp. 201–210.

Feller, Robert L., and Catherine W. Bailie. "Solubility of Aged Coatings Based on Dammar, Mastic and Resin AW-2," *Bulletin of the American Group—IIC,* 12:2 (April 1972), pp. 72–81.

Feller, Robert L., and J.J. Matous. "Critical Pigment Volume Concentration and Chalking in Paints," *Bulletin of the American Group—IIC,* 5:1 (October 1964), pp. 25–26.

Gettens, Rutherford J. "Identification of Pigments and Inerts on Paintings and Other Museum Objects." In *Application of Science in the Examination of Works of Art; Proceedings of the Seminar: September 15–18, 1958* (Boston: Museum of Fine Arts, 1959), pp. 31–50.

Gettens, Rutherford J. "Proposal for a Handbook on Analysis of Materials of Paintings." In *Recent Advances in Conservation* (London: Butterworths, 1963), pp. 26–28.

Gettens, Rutherford J.; Robert L. Feller; and W.T. Chase. "Identification of the Materials of Painting: Vermilion and Cinnabar," *Studies in Conservation,* 17:2 (May 1972), pp. 45–69. ◆ Sources, preparation, physical characteristics, color and spectral reflection, criteria for identification, notable occurrences.

Gettens, Rutherford J., and Elizabeth W. Fitzhugh. "Identification of the Materials of Painting: Azurite and Blue Verditer," *Studies in Conservation,* 11:2 (May 1966), pp. 54–61. ◆ Source, composition, preparation, particle, optical and chemical properties, permanence, tests.

Gettens, Rutherford J., and Elizabeth W. Fitzhugh. "Identification of the Materials of Painting: Malachite and Green Verditer," *Studies in Conservation,* 19:1 (February 1974), pp. 2–23. ◆ Composition, sources, history of use, particle, chemical and optical properties, permanence, tests, criteria for identification.

Gettens, Rutherford J., and Frank W. Sterner. "The Compatibility of Pigments in Artists' Oil Paints," *Technical Studies in the*

Field of the Fine Arts, X:1 (July 1941), pp. 18–28.

Gettens, Rutherford J., and George L. Stout. *Painting Materials: A Short Encyclopedia.* 1942. Reprint. New York: Dover Publications, 1966. 333 pp., illus., glossary, bibliog., paperback. ◆ A reliable source of information on materials used as supports, grounds, pigments, media, adhesives, varnishes and solvents and on equipment and tools, in painting past and present. A valuable reference for professional conservators and research scholars.

Gettens, Rutherford J.; Hermann Kühn; and W.T. Chase. "Identification of the Materials of Painting: Lead White," *Studies in Conservation,* 12:4 (November 1967), pp. 125–139. ◆ Composition, source, preparation, history of use, relationship to mediums, particle, optical and chemical properties, permanence and compatibility, criteria for identification, notable occurrences.

Harley, Rosamond D. *Artists' Pigments, c.1600–1835: A Study in English Documentary Sources.* New York: American Elsevier Publishing Co., Inc., 1970. 230 pp., illus., bibliog.

Heaton, Noel. *Outlines of Paint Technology; with Additional Notes by L.R. Hickson.* 3rd ed. London: Charles Griffin & Co., Ltd., 1956. 467 pp., illus., bibliog.

Hendy, Philip, and A.S. Lucas. "The Ground in Pictures," *Museum,* XXI:4 (1968), pp. 266–276.

Herberts, Kurt. *The Complete Book of Artists' Techniques.* New York: Praeger Publishers, 1969. 352 pp., illus., bibliog., appendix.

Hiler, Hilaire. *Notes on the Technique of Painting.* 3rd ed. New York: Watson-Guptill Publications, 1969. 347 pp., illus., bibliog.

Jensen, Lawrence N. *Synthetic Painting Media.* Englewood Cliffs, N.J.: Prentice-Hall, 1964. 138 pp., illus., bibliog.

Keck, Caroline, and H.W. Williams. "A Mid-Eighteenth Century French Apprentice Painter's Note-Book," *Technical Studies in the Field of the Fine Arts,* LX:2 (October 1946), pp. 105–112.

Keck, Sheldon. "A Use of Infra-Red Photography in the Study of Technique," *Technical Studies in the Field of the Fine Arts,* IX:3 (January 1941), pp. 145–152.

Kühn, Hermann. "Identification of the Materials of Painting: Lead-Tin Yellow," *Studies in Conservation,* 13:1 (February 1968), pp. 7–33. ◆ Composition, history of use, occurrences, optical, chemical and pigment properties, criteria for identification.

Kühn, Hermann. "Identification of the Materials of Painting: Verdigris and Copper Resinate," *Studies in Conservation,* 15:1 (February 1970), pp. 12–36. ◆ Preparation, chemical composition and properties, particle characteristics, pigment properties, microchemical tests, criteria for identification.

Lamb, Lynton. *Materials and Methods of Painting.* New York: Oxford University Press, 1970. 112 pp., illus., bibliog., index.

Laurie, Arthur P. *The Painter's Methods and Materials.* 1926. Reprint. New York: Dover Publications, 1967. 249 pp., illus.

Laurie, Arthur P. *Pigments and Mediums of the Old Masters, With a Special Chapter on Microphotographic Study of Brushwork.* London: Macmillan & Co., 1914. 192 pp., illus.

Laurie, Arthur P. *The Technique of the Great Painters: History of Painting Materials from Early Egypt to the Present Day.* London: Carroll & Nicholson, 1949. 192 pp., illus.

Lyman, John. "Paper as a Ground for Oil Painting," *Technical Studies in the Field of the Fine Arts,* I:4 (April 1933), pp. 207–211.

Malaguzzi-Valerj, Valerio. "Ancient Fresco Technique in the Light of Scientific Examination." In *Application of Science in the Examination of Works of Art; Proceedings of the Seminar: June 15–19, 1970* (Boston: Museum of Fine Arts, 1973), pp. 164–170.

Martens, Charles R. *Emulsion and Water-Soluble Paints and Coatings.* New York: Reinhold Publishing Corp., 1964. 160 pp., illus., bibliog.

Martin, John H., and W.M. Morgans. *Guide to Pigments and to Varnish and Lacquer*

Constituents. London: Leonard Hill, 1954. 127 pp.

Materials: A Scientific American Book. San Francisco: W.H. Freeman, 1967. 210 pp., illus., bibliog., paperback.

Mayer, Ralph. *The Artist's Handbook of Materials and Techniques.* 3rd ed. New York: Viking Press, 1970. 750 pp., illus., bibliog.

Mayer, Ralph. "Some Notes on Nineteenth Century Canvas Makers," *Technical Studies in the Field of the Fine Arts,* X:3 (January 1932), pp. 131–137.

Merrifield, Mary P. *The Art of Fresco Painting, As Practiced by the Old Italian and Spanish Masters, with a Preliminary Inquiry into the Nature of the Colours Used in Fresco Painting, with Observations and Notes.* London: A. Tiranti, 1952. 134 pp., illus. ◆ First edition published in 1846.

Merrifield, Mary P. *Original Treatises on the Arts of Painting.* 1849. Reprint. New York: Dover Publications, 1967. 2 vols., bibliog.

Mills, John Fitzmaurice. *Acrylic Painting.* London: I. Pitman, 1965. 126 pp., illus. ◆ Techniques of using acrylic paints.

Mühlethaler, Bruno, and Jean Thissen. "Identification of the Materials of Painting: Smalt," *Studies in Conservation,* 14:2 (May 1969), pp. 47–61. ◆ Composition, preparation, history of use, particle, optical, and pigment properties, chemical properties, occurrences, criteria for identification.

Nathans, Jerome. "Colourmen's Stencils," *Remembrances of Passaic County,* no. 2 (1972). 4 pp. ◆ Discusses the implications of canvas makers' and dealers' trade stamps found on reverse of some nineteenth century American paintings.

Paint Testing Manual; Physical and Chemical Examination of Paints, Varnishes, Lacquers and Colors. Edited by G.G. Sward. 13th ed. Philadelphia: American Society for Testing and Materials, 1972. 599 pp., illus., graphs, charts, drawings, footnotes, index.

Patton, Temple C. *Pigment Handbook.* New York: John Wiley & Sons, 1973. 3 vols., bibliog. references. ◆ Vol. 1: *Properties and Economics;* Vol. 2: *Applications and Markets;* Vol. 3: *Characterization and Physical Relationships.*

Plesters, Joyce. "Identification of the Materials of Painting: Ultramarine Blue, Natural and Artificial," *Studies in Conservation,* 11:2 (May 1966), pp. 63–91. ◆ Composition, sources, preparation, particle, optical, pigment and chemical properties, criteria for identification, notable occurrences.

Pomerantz, Louis. *Is Your Contemporary Painting More Temporary Than You Think? Vital Technical Information for the Present-Day Artist.* Chicago: International Book Co., 1967. 62 pp., illus.

Quandt, Eleanor S. "Observations Concerning the Application of Grounds in 18th Century American Paintings," *Bulletin of the American Group—IIC* 12:1 (1971), pp. 37–43.

Rawlins, F. Ian G. "The Optical Properties of Some Common Varnishes," *Technical Studies in the Field of the Fine Arts,* VI:3 (January 1938), pp. 180–182.

Rawlins, F. Ian G., and George L. Stout. "Brief Methods of Describing Paint," *Technical Studies in the Field of the Fine Arts,* X:1 (July 1941), pp. 37–46.

Ross, Janet L. "A Note on the Use of Mosaic Gold," *Studies in Conservation,* 18:4 (November 1973), pp. 174–176.

Ruhemann, Helmut. "A Tentative Scheme for Analysis of Painting Technique," *Technical Studies in the Field of the Fine Arts,* X:2 (October 1941), pp. 73–98.

Sayre, Edward V. "Investigation of Italian Frescoes, Their Materials, Deterioration and Treatment." In *Application of Science in the Examination of Works of Art; Proceedings of the Seminar: June 15–19, 1970* (Boston: Museum of Fine Arts, 1973), pp. 176–181.

Shell Oil Company. *Paint.* Film, 25 minutes, 16 mm., sound, color, free rental, (1967). ◆ Shows the materials, tools and techniques of painting and paint-making from cave painters on. Available from the Shell Film Library, 450 North Meridian Street, Indianapolis, Indiana 46204.

Staccioli, G., and Umberto Tamburini. "Ageing of Wood: Preliminary Studies of Panel Paintings." In *Application of Science in* the *Examination of Works of Art; Proceedings of the Seminar: June 15–19, 1970* (Boston: Museum of Fine Arts, 1973), pp. 235–237.

Stout, George L. "Classes of Simple Paint Structure," *Technical Studies in the Field of the Fine Arts,* VI:4 (April 1938), pp. 221–239.

Stout, George L. "The Grip of the Artist's Brush," *Technical Studies in the Field of the Fine Arts,* X:1 (July 1941), pp. 3–17.

Stout, George L. "One Aspect of the So-called 'Mixed Technique'," *Technical Studies in the Field of the Fine Arts,* VII:2 (October 1938), pp. 59–72.

Stout, George L. "A Study of the Method in a Flemish Painting," *Technical Studies in the Field of the Fine Arts,* I:4 (April 1933), pp. 181–206.

Taubes, Frederic. *The Art and Technique of Oil Painting.* New York: Dodd, Mead & Co., 1957. 113 pp., illus.

Thompson, Daniel V. *The Materials and Techniques of Medieval Painting.* 1936. Reprint. New York: Dover Publications, 1956. 239 pp., bibliog. notes, index, paper. ◆ Also available from Peter Smith.

Thomson, Garry. "New Picture Varnishes." In *Recent Advances in Conservation* (London: Butterworths, 1963), pp. 176–184.

Thomson, Garry. "Some Picture Varnishes," *Studies in Conservation,* 3:2 (October 1957), pp. 64–79.

Toch, Maximilian. *How to Paint Permanent Pictures.* New York: D. Van Nostrand Co., 1922. 105 pp.

Toch, Maximilian. *Materials for Permanent Painting: A Manual for Manufacturers, Art Dealers, Artists and Collectors.* New York: Van Nostrand Co., 1911. 208 pp.

Toch, Maximilian. *Paint, Paintings and Restoration.* Rev. ed. New York: D. Van Nostrand Co., Inc., 1931. 189 pp., illus., bibliog.

"Trial Data on Painting Materials—Mediums, Adhesives, and Film Substances," *Technical Studies in the Field of the Fine Arts,* VI:1 (July 1937), pp. 26–68; VI:2 (October 1937), pp. 111–145.

"Trial Data on Painting Materials—Pigments and Inert Materials," *Technical*

Studies in the Field of the Fine Arts, VII:4 (April 1939), pp. 200–243.

"Trial Data on Painting Materials—Solvents, Dilutents, and Detergents," *Technical Studies in the Field of the Fine Arts,* IX:4 (April 1941), pp. 221–252.

"Trial Data on Painting Materials—Tools and Equipment," *Technical Studies in the Field of the Fine Arts,* IX:1 (July 1940), pp. 25–71.

Turner, Gerald P.A. *Introduction to Paint Chemistry.* London: Chapman & Hall, 1967. 244 pp., tables, diagrams, bibliog.

Van Schendel, A.F.E. "Manufacture of Vermilion in 17th Century Amsterdam—The Pekstok Papers," *Studies in Conservation,* 17:2 (May 1972), pp. 70–82. ◆ A description of procedures and personal experience in making vermilion according to the Dutch process.

Von Fischer, William, ed. *Paint and Varnish Technology.* 1948. Reprint. New York: Hafner, 1964. 509 pp., illus., bibliog.

Watrous, James. *The Craft of Old-Master Drawings.* Madison, Wisc.: University of Wisconsin Press, 1957. 170 pp., illus. ◆ Explains the techniques, tools and materials of old prints and drawings.

Wild, Angenitus Martinus De. *The Scientific Examination of Pictures: An Investigation of the Pigments Used by Dutch and Flemish Masters from the Brothers Van Eyck to the Middle of the 19th Century.* London: G. Bell & Sons, Ltd., 1929. 105 pp., illus., bibliog. footnotes.

Woody, Russell O., Jr. *Polymer Painting and Related Techniques; with Course Outline and Works of Prominent Artists.* New York: Van Nostrand Reinhold Co., 1969. 108 pp., illus., paperback.

Examination and Analysis of Paintings

Barnes, Norman F. "A Spectrophotometric Study of Artists' Pigments," *Technical Studies in the Field of the Fine Arts,* VII:3 (January 1939), pp. 120–138.

Birks, L.S. *Electron Probe Microanalysis.* 2nd ed. New York: Wiley-Interscience Publishers, 1971. 190 pp., illus., bibliog. references.

Bradley, Morton C., Jr. "Systems of Color Classification," *Technical Studies in the Field of the Fine Arts,* VI:4 (April 1938), pp. 240–276.

Bridgman, Charles F. "Use of Radiation in Philately and in Examination of Paintings." In *The Science of Ionizing Radiation* (Springfield, Ill.: C.C. Thomas, 1965), pp. 655–681.

Bridgman, Charles F., and Lou Gibson. "Infrared Luminescence in the Photographic Examination of Paintings and Other Art Objects," *Studies in Conservation,* 8:3 (August 1963), pp. 77–83.

Bridgman, Charles F., and Sheldon Keck. "The Radiography of Paintings," *Medical Radiography and Photography,* 37:3 (1961), pp. 62–70. ◆ Explains to a medical radiologist how to adjust and adapt his equipment in order to make successful radiographs of art objects.

Bridgman, Charles.; Sheldon Keck; and Harold F. Sherwood. "The Radiography of Panel Paintings by Electron Emission," *Studies in Conservation,* 3:4 (October 1958), pp. 175–182.

Brommelle, Norman. "Colour and Conservation," *Studies in Conservation,* 2:2 (October 1955), pp. 76–85.

Buck, Richard. "On Conservation: Analytical Systems," *Museum News,* 52:6 (March 1974), pp. 16; 18–19. ◆ Includes charts on various types of analysis, indicating application, sample size and type, purpose, and availability.

Buck, Richard. "On Conservation: Use of Infrared, Ultraviolet and X-Ray in Scientific Examination and Analysis," *Museum News,* 52:5 (January-February 1974), pp. 20; 23–24; 26.

Buck, Richard D., and Robert L. Feller. "The Examination and Treatment of a Fayum Portrait." In *Conservation of Paintings and the Graphic Arts* (London: International Institute for Conservation of Historic and Artistic Works, 1972), pp. 801–808.

Buck, Richard D., and George L. Stout. "Original and Later Paint in Pictures," *Technical Studies in the Field of the Fine Arts,* VIII:3 (January 1940), pp. 123–150.

Butler, Marigene H. "Application of the Polarizing Microscope in the Conservation of Paintings and Other Works of Art," *Bulletin of the American Group—IIC,* 11:2 (April 1971), pp. 107–119.

Butler, Marigene H. *Polarized Light Microscopy in the Conservation of Painting.* Chicago: The Art Institute of Chicago, 1970. 17 pp., illus., diagrams, paperback. ◆ Available from the Art Institute of Chicago, Conservation Department, Michigan Avenue at Adams Street, Chicago, Illinois 60603, and Intermuseum Laboratory, Allen Art Building, Oberlin, Ohio 44074.

Clark, Walter. *Photography by Infra-Red, Its Principles and Applications.* 2nd ed. New York: J. Wiley & Sons, Inc., 1946. 472 pp., illus., plans, diagrams, bibliog. ◆ Principles practices and application, including a section on infrared photography of pictures and documents.

Dodds, Leonard V. "Examination of Documents and Paintings," *Art and Archaeology,* 30:1–2 (July–August 1930), pp. 31–35; 52.

Eastman Kodak Company. *Infrared and Ultraviolet Photography.* 1st comb. ed. Rochester, N.Y.: Eastman Kodak Co., 1972. 88 pp., illus., bibliog.

Elzinga-Ter Haar, G. "On the Use of the Electron Microprobe in Analysis of Cross-Sections of Paint Samples," *Studies in Conservation,* 16:2 (May 1971), pp. 41–55.

Farnsworth, Marie. "Infra-Red Absorption of Paint Materials," *Technical Studies in the Field of the Fine Arts,* VII:2 (October 1938), pp. 88–98.

Feller, Robert L. "Color Change in Oil Paintings." Reprinted from *Carnegie Magazine,* October 1954. 6 pp., illus., references.

Feller, Robert L. "Problems in Reflectance Spectrophotometry." In *Contributions to the London Conference on Museum Climatology* (London: International Institute for Conservation, 1968), pp. 257–269.

Gettens, Rutherford J. "The Cross-Sectioning of Paint Films," *Technical Studies in the Field of the Fine Arts,* V:1 (July 1936), pp. 18–22.

Gettens, Rutherford J. "An Equipment for the Microchemical Examination of Pictures and Other Works of Art," *Technical Studies in the Field of the Fine Arts,* II:4 (April 1934), pp. 185–202.

Gettens, Rutherford J. "A Microsectioner for Paint Films," *Technical Studies in the Field of the Fine Arts,* I:1 (July 1932), pp. 20–28.

Giovanoli, Rudolph, and Bruno Mühlethaler. "Investigation of Discoloured Smalt," *Studies in Conservation,* 15:1 (February 1970), pp. 37–44.

Hall, E.T. "Methods of Analysis (Physical and Microchemical) Applied to Paintings and Antiquities." In *Recent Advances in Conservation* (London: Butterworths, 1963), pp. 29–32. ◆ Includes comparative merits of various types of analytical procedures: standard wet chemistry, optical emission spectrometry, x-ray fluorescent spectrometry, x-ray diffraction, electron probe microanalysis.

Hanlan, J.F. "The EDX Spectrometer in Musem Use," *Bulletin of the American Group—IIC,* (April 1971), pp. 85–90.

Hanlan, J.F.; Nathan Stolow; J. Mac G. Grant; and R.W. Tolinie. "Applications of Non-Dispersive X-Ray Fluorescence Analyses to the Study of Works of Art," *Bulletin of the American Group—IIC,* 10:2 (April 1970), pp. 25–40.

Heiber, W. "The Use of an Infra-Red Image-Converter for the Examination of Panel Paintings," *Studies in Conservation,* 13:3 (August 1968), pp. 145–149.

Hey, Margaret. "The Analysis of Paint Media by Paper Chromatography," *Studies in Conservation,* 3:4 (October 1958), pp. 183–193.

Hulehrnreich, E.G. Van't. "Infrared Microspectroscopy for the Analysis of Old Painting Materials," *Studies in Conservation,* 15:3 (August 1970), pp. 175–182.

Johnson, Meryl, and Elisabeth Packard. "Methods Used for the Identification of Binding Media in Italian Painting of the Fifteenth and Sixteenth Centuries," *Studies in Conservation,* 16:4 (November 1971), pp. 145–164.

Jones, Peter Lloyd. "Some Observations on Methods for Identifying Proteins in Paint Media," *Studies in Conservation,* 7:1 (February 1962), pp. 10–16.

Keck, Sheldon. "Mechanical Alteration of the Paint Film," *Studies in Conservation,* 14:1 (February 1969), pp. 9–30. ◆ Discusses deterioration of paintings caused by chemical, physical and biological agents, both internal and external.

Keck, Sheldon. "Photographic Recording of the Condition of Paintings," *Museum News,* 25:15 (February 1948), pp. 7–8.

Keck, Sheldon. "Radiation and Optical Techniques in the Visual Examination of Paintings." Reprinted from *Applied Optics,* 8:1 (January 1969), pp. 41–48.

Keck, Sheldon. "A Use of Infra-Red Photography in the Study of Technique," *Technical Studies in the Field of the Fine Arts,* 9:3 (January 1941), pp. 145–152.

Keck, Sheldon, and Robert L. Feller. "Detection of an Epoxy-Resin Coating on a Seventeenth-Century Painting," *Studies in Conservation,* 9:1 (February 1964), pp. 1–8.

Keck, Sheldon, and Theodore Peters, Jr. "Identification of Protein-Containing Paint Media by Quantitative Amino Acid Analysis," *Studies in Conservation,* 14:2 (May 1969), pp. 75–82. ◆ Application of quantitative amino acid assay was found to be a useful and accurate means of determining the nature of protein media when sufficient material was present.

Keisch, Bernard. "On the Use of Isotope Mass Spectrometry in the Identification of Artists' Pigments," *Studies in Conservation,* 15:1 (February 1970), pp. 1–11.

Kelly, Kenneth L. *A Universal Color Language.* Technical Abstracts. New York: n.p., c 1965. 7 pp. ◆ Reprint from *Color Engineering,* March-April, 1965.

Kühn, Hermann. "Detection and Identification of Waxes Including Punic Wax, by Infra-Red Spectrography," *Studies in Conservation,* 5:2 (May 1960), pp. 71–81.

Kühn, Hermann. "Trace Elements in White Lead and Their Determination by Emission Spectrum and Neutron Activation Analysis," *Studies in Conservation,* 11:4 (November 1966), pp. 163–169.

Kühn, Hermann, and Christel Zocher. "Feature Cards for the Storing of Technical

Data Which Result from the Scientific Examination of Works of Art," *Studies in Conservation,* 15:2 (May 1970), pp. 102–121.

Locke, David C., and Orrin H. Riley. "Chemical Analysis of Paint Samples Using the Weisz Ring Oven Technique," *Studies in Conservation,* 15:2 (May 1970), pp. 94–101. ♦ A rapid and sensitive yet simple method for the qualitative analysis of pigments and other inorganic materials of interest in conservation.

London. National Gallery. Laboratory. *From the National Gallery Laboratory.* London: Printed for the Trustees, 1940. 50 pp., illus. ♦ Demonstrates the use of x-rays and ether waves in the examination of paintings.

Lyon, R. Arcadius. "Infra-Red Radiations Aid Examinations of Paintings," *Technical Studies in the Field of the Fine Arts,* II:4 (April 1934), pp. 203–212.

Majewski, Lawrence J. "Interim Report of an Investigation of Processes of Disintegration of Frescoes." In *Application of Science in the Examination of Works of Art; Proceedings of the Seminar: June 15–19, 1970* (Boston: Museum of Fine Arts, 1973), pp. 182–185.

Mates, Robert E. *Photographing Art.* Philadelphia: Chilton Books, 1966. 128 pp., illus., bibliog. ♦ Techniques used by a museum staff photographer to photograph paintings, drawings, watercolors, collages, sculpture, and a variety of art objects.

Mills, John S. "The Gas Chromatographic Examination of Paint Media, Part I: Fatty Acid Composition and Identification of Dried Oil Films," *Studies in Conservation,* 11:2 (May 1966), pp. 92–107.

Minneapolis Institute of Arts. *Fakes and Forgeries.* Minneapolis: The Institute, 1973. unpaged, illus., bibliog. ♦ Catalogue of an exhibition at the Minneapolis Institute of Arts, July 11 to September 29, 1973.

Munsell, Albert H. *A Color Notation: An Illustrated System Defining All Colors and Their Relations by Measured Scales of Hue, Value, and Chroma.* 12th ed., edited and rearranged. Baltimore: Munsell Color Co., Inc., c 1946, 1971. 67 pp., photos, diagrams, graphs, tables, glossary, appendices, index, insert color charts with color chips. ♦ Describes the principles of color order, color nota-

tion and color balance. A standard student text.

Munsell Color Company, Inc., Baltimore. *Munsell Book of Color; Matte Finish Collection.* Neighboring Hues ed. Baltimore: Munsell Color Co., Inc., 1967. 1 vol., chiefly illus., looseleaf. ♦ A standard guide for the differentiation and notation of color hues and values. Available from Munsell Color Company, 2441 North Calvert Street, Baltimore, Maryland 21218.

Munsell Color Company, Inc., Baltimore. *Munsell Book of Color; Glossy Finish Collection.* Baltimore: Munsell Color Co., Inc., 1966. 2 parts, looseleaf. ♦ A standard guide for the differentiation and notation of color hues and values. Available from Munsell Color Company, 2441 North Calvert Street, Baltimore, Maryland 21218.

Olin, C.H., and T.G. Carter. "Infrared Photography of Painting Materials." In *IIC— American Group Technical Papers from 1968 through 1970* (New York: IIC-AG, 1970), pp. 83–88.

Plenderleith, Harold J. "Notes on Technique in the Examination of Panel Paintings," *Technical Studies in the Field of the Fine Arts,* I:1 (July 1932), pp. 3–7.

Plesters, Joyce. "A Preliminary Note on the Incidence of Discolouration of Smalt in Oil Media," *Studies in Conservation,* 14:2 (May 1969), pp. 62–74.

Rawlins, F. Ian G. "Physical Factors in X-Ray Photography," *Technical Studies in the Field of the Fine Arts,* VII:2 (October 1938), pp. 73–79.

Rawlins, F. Ian G. "Studies in the Colorimetry of Paintings, I," *Technical Studies in the Field of the Fine Arts,* IV:4 (April 1936), pp. 179–186.

Rawlins, F. Ian G. "Studies in the Colorimetry of Paintings, II," *Technical Studies in the Field of the Fine Arts,* V:3 (January 1937), pp. 150–156.

Rawlins, F. Ian G. "Studies in the Colorimetry of Paintings, III," *Technical Studies in the Field of the Fine Arts,* IX:4 (April 1941), pp. 207–220.

Rawlins, F. Ian G. "Studies in the Colorimetry of Paintings—A Note in Conclusion,"

Technical Studies in the Field of the Fine Arts, X:4 (April 1942), pp. 230–231.

Ridgway, Robert. *Color Standards and Color Nomenclature.* Washington, D.C.: The Author, 1912. 47 pp., illus.

Robertson, Clements L. "The Visual and Optical Examination of Works of Art," *Museum News,* 46:4 (December 1967), Technical Supplement no. 20.

Rorimer, James J. *Ultra-Violet Rays and Their Use in the Examination of Works of Art.* New York: Metropolitan Museum of Art, 1931. 61 pp., diagrams, bibliog.

Rosen, David, and Henry Marceau. "A Study in the Use of Photographs in the Identification of Paintings," *Technical Studies in the Field of the Fine Arts,* VI:2 (October 1937), pp. 75–87.

Ruhemann, Helmut. "Criteria for Distinguishing Additions from Original Paint," *Studies in Conservation,* 3:4 (October 1958), pp. 145–161.

Salmon, Maurice E. "An X-Ray Fluorescence Method for Micro-Samples." In *Application of Science in the Examination of Works of Art; Proceedings of the Seminar June 15–19, 1970* (Boston: Museum of Fine Arts, 1973), pp. 31–37. ◆ See also: *IIC—American Group Technical Papers from 1968 through 1970* (New York: IIC-AG, 1970), pp. 31–46.

Sayre, Edward V., and Heather N. Lechtman. "Neutron Activation Autoradiography of Oil Paintings," *Studies in Conservation,* 13:4 (November 1968), pp. 161–185.

Stolow, Nathan; James F. Hanlan; and Raymond Boyer. "Element Distribution in Cross-Sections of Paintings Studied by the X-Ray Macroprobe," *Studies in Conservation,* 14:4 (November 1969), pp. 139–151.

Stout, George L. "General Notes on the Condition of Paintings—A Brief Outline for Purposes of Record," *Technical Studies in the Field of the Fine Arts,* VII:3 (January 1939), pp. 159–166.

Stout, George L., and Harry F. Cross. "Properties of Surface Films," *Technical Studies in the Field of the Fine Arts,* V:4 (April 1937), pp. 241–249.

Van Asperen de Boer, J.R.J. "Reflectog-raphy of Painting Using an Infra-Red Vidicon Television System," *Studies in Conservation,* 14:3 (August 1969), pp. 96–118. ◆ A method of improving the detectability of underdrawings in medieval paintings.

Weiss, Norman R., and H. Biemann. "Application of Mass Spectrometric Techniques to the Differentiation of Paint Media." In *Conservation of Paintings and the Graphic Arts* (London: International Institute for Conservation of Historic and Artistic Works, 1972), pp. 729–800.

Winterthur Conference on Museum Operation and Connoisseurship, 17th, 1971. *American Painting to 1776: A Reappraisal.* Edited by Ian M.G. Quimby. Charlottesville, Va.: University Press of Virginia, 1971. 384 pp., illus., bibliog. references. ◆ The second part of this book discusses the technical means of identifying paintings, i.e., the recording of evidence, radiography as an aid to examination, the analysis of paint pigments and other processes.

Young, W.J. "Application of the Electron Microbeam Probe and Micro X-Rays in Non-Destructive Analysis." In *Recent Advances in Conservation* (London: Butterworths, 1963), pp. 33–38.

Young. W.J. "Application of the Laser and Electron Microbeam Probe in Analyses." In *IIC—American Group Technical Papers from 1968 through 1970* (New York: IIC-AG, 1970), pp. 59–62.

Techniques of Conservation and Restoration

Althofer, Heinz. "The Use of Polyethylene Glycols in the Field of Painting Restoration," *Studies in Conservation,* 4:1 (February 1959), pp. 31–34.

Asmus, J.F., et al. *Venetian Art Preservation Via Holography.* LaJolla, Calif.: Science Applications, Inc., 1972. 63 pp., illus.

Beaufort, Thomas R. *Pictures and How to Clean Them; To Which Are Added Notes on Things Useful in Restoration Work.* London: John Land, 1926. 202 pp., illus., diagrams, bibliog.

Berger, Gustav A. "Application of Heat Activated Adhesives for the Consolidation of

Paintings," *Bulletin of the American Group—IIC*, 11:2 (April 1971), pp. 124–128.

Berger, Gustav A. "Formulating Adhesives for the Conservation of Paintings." In *Conservation of Paintings and the Graphic Arts* (London: International Institute for Conservation of Historic and Artistic Works, 1972), pp. 613–630.

Berger, Gustav A. "A New Adhesive for the Consolidation of Paintings, Drawings and Textiles," *Bulletin of the American Group—IIC*, 11:1 (October 1970), pp. 36–38.

Berger, Gustav A. "Reflections on a Vaseline Jar," *Bulletin of the American Group—IIC*, 6:1 (April 1966), pp. 3–5. ♦ Discusses the problem of matching color in inpainting.

Berger, Gustav A. "Some Effects of Impregnating Adhesives on Paint Film," *Bulletin of the American Group—IIC*, 12:2 (April 1972), pp. 25–47.

Berger, Gustav A. "The Testing of Adhesives for the Consolidation of Painting." In *IIC—American Group Technical Papers from 1968 through 1970* (New York: IIC-AG, 1970), pp. 63–77. ♦ Describes tests on mechanical performance of various adhesives; adhesion to paint films; adhesion to conventional and newly developed lining supports; cold flow of lining adhesives; rigidity of lining laminates. See also: *Studies in Conservation*, 17:4 (November 1972), pp. 173–194.

Berger, Gustav A. "Weave Interference in Vacuum Lining of Pictures," *Studies in Conservation*, 11:4 (November 1966), pp. 170–180.

Bhowmik, Swarna Kamal. "A Non-Aqueous Method for the Restoration of Indian Miniature Paintings," *Studies in Conservation*, 12:3 (August 1967), pp. 116–120.

Boissonnas, Alain G. "The Treatment of Fire Blistered Oil Paintings," *Studies in Conservation*, 8:2 (May 1963), pp. 55–66.

Boustead, William. "The Conservation and Restoration of Easel Paintings." In *The Conservation of Cultural Property with Special Reference to Tropical Conditions* (Paris: UNESCO, 1968), pp. 191–208. ♦ Includes paintings on wood panels, glass covers, paintings in desert climates, watercolors.

Buck, Richard D. "Some Applications of Mechanics to the Treatment of Panel Paint-

ings." In *Recent Advances in Conservation* (London: Butterworths, 1963), pp. 156–162.

Buck, Richard D. "Some Applications of Rheology to the Treatment of Panel Paintings," *Studies in Conservation*, 17:1 (February 1972), pp. 1–11. ♦ A survey of some properties of wood related to dimensional stability. Warping, bending, elasticity, plasticity, moisture and rheological behavior discussed briefly.

Buck, Richard D. "The Use of Moisture Barriers on Panel Paintings," *Studies in Conservation*, 6:1 (February 1961), pp. 9–20.

Buck, Richard D., and Robert L. Feller. "The Examination and Treatment of a Fayum Portrait." In *Conservation of Paintings and the Graphic Arts* (London: International Institute for Conservation of Historic and Artistic Works, 1972), pp. 801–808.

Buck, Richard D., and R. Merrill. "Honeycomb Core Construction for Supporting Panels," *Bulletin of the American Group—IIC*, 12:2 (April 1972), pp. 62–67.

Church of England. Central Council of Diocesan Advisory Committees for the Care of Churches. *The Conservation of English Wall Paintings; Being a Report of a Committee Set Up by the Central Council for the Care of Churches and the Society for the Protection of Ancient Buildings*. London: Central Council for the Care of Churches, 1959. 30 pp., illus.

Colonial Williamsburg, Film Distribution Section. *The Art of the Conservator*. With Russell J. Quandt and Robert Feller. Film, 57 minutes, 16 mm., color, sound (1966); and, 28½ minutes, 16 mm., color, sound (1972). ♦ Explains methods and reasoning used by conservators. Shows investigative techniques, relining, cleaning, filling and inpainting.

Cornelius, F. DuPont. "Further Developments in the Treatment of Fire-Blistered Oil Paintings," *Studies in Conservation*, 11:1 (February 1966), pp. 31–36.

Courtais, Henri G. "A Blind Approach to the Removal of a Fresco," *Studies in Conservation*, 8:1 (February 1963), pp. 10–31.

Cursiter, Stanley, and A. Martin De Wild. "A Note on Picture Relining," *Technical Studies in the Field of the Fine Arts*, VI:3 (January 1938), pp. 175–179.

Cursiter, Stanley, and A. Martin De Wild. "Picture Relining," *Technical Studies in the Field of the Fine Arts,* V:3 (January 1937), pp. 157–178.

Cursiter, Stanley, and A. Martin De Wild. "Picture Relining," *Technical Studies in the Field of the Fine Arts,* VII:4 (April 1939), pp. 191–195.

Cursiter, Stanley, and A. Martin De Wild. "Picture Relining with Wax," *Technical Studies in the Field of the Fine Arts,* VII:2 (October 1938), pp. 80–87.

Feller, Robert L. "Notes on the Chemistry of Bleaching," *Bulletin of the American Group—IIC,* 11:2 (April 1971), pp. 39–75.

Feller, Robert L. "Problems in Retouching: Chalking of Intermedial Layers," *Bulletin of the American Group—IIC,* 7:1 (October 1966), pp. 32–34.

Freer Gallery of Art. *The Art of the Hyogushi.* Film, 45 minutes, 16 mm., color, sound (1973). ◆ The hyogushi treat three Japanese paintings. The processes shown include cutting the paintings from their old mounts, washing, drying, reinforcing cracks, filling holes, applying backing papers, retouching and constructing the new supports.

Gettens, Rutherford J. "Preliminary Report on the Measurement of the Moisture Permeability of Protective Coatings," *Technical Studies in the Field of the Fine Arts,* I:2 (October 1932), pp. 63–68.

Gettens, Rutherford J., and Elizabeth Bigelow. "The Moisture Permeability of Protective Coatings," *Technical Studies in the Field of the Fine Arts,* II:1 (July 1933), pp. 15–25.

Gettens, Rutherford J.; Murray Pease; and George L. Stout. "The Problem of Mould Growth in Paintings," *Technical Studies in the Field of the Fine Arts,* IX:3 (January 1941). pp. 127–144.

Harris, Nancy E., and Lawrence J. Majewski. "The Examination and Treatment of a Fresco Fragment from Teotihuacan," *Bulletin of the American Institute for Conservation of Historic and Artistic Works,* 13:2 (1973), pp. 105–113.

Hatch, Aram H. "Notes on the Experimental Studies Made for the Prevention of Mold Growth on Mural Paintings," *Technical Studies in the Field of the Fine Arts,* II:3 (January 1934), pp. 129–138.

Hess, Manfred, et al., eds. *Paint Film Defects, Their Causes and Cure.* 2nd ed., completely revised. New York: Reinhold Publishing Corp., 1965. 604 pp., illus., bibliog.

Hulmer, Eric C. "Notes on the Formulation and Application of Acrylic Coatings." In *Conservation of Paintings and the Graphic Arts* (London: International Institute for Conservation of Historic and Artistic Works, 1972), pp. 211–214. ◆ See also: *Bulletin of the American Group—IIC,* 11:2 (April 1971), pp. 132–139.

Hulmer, Eric C. "Notes on the Formulation and Application of Adhesives and Supports," *Bulletin of the American Group—IIC,* 12:1 (1971), pp. 46–54.

ICOM Commission for the Care of Paintings. "The Care of Paintings: The Care of Wood Panels," *Museum,* VIII:3 (1955), entire issue.

ICOM Commission for the Care of Paintings. "The Care of Paintings: Fabric Paint Supports," *Museum,* XIII:3 (1960), pp. 134–171.

Jones, Elizabeth H. "The Effect of Ageing and Re-Forming on the Ease of Solubility of Certain Resins." In *Recent Advances in Conservation* (London: Butterworths, 1963), pp. 79–83.

Keck, Sheldon. "On the Conservation of Early American Painting," *Antiques,* 53:1 (January 1948), pp. 52–54.

Keck, Sheldon. "The Transfer of a Small Icon to a Support of Vinyl Resin," *Technical Studies in the Field of the Fine Arts,* 9:1 (July 1940), pp. 11–20.

Kostrov, P.I. and E.G. Sheinina. "Restoration of Monumental Painting on Loess Plaster Using Synthetic Resins," *Studies in Conservation,* 6:2–3 (August 1961), pp. 90–106.

Lank, Herbert. "The Use of Dimethyl Formamide Vapour in Reforming Blanched Oil Paintings." In *Conservation of Paintings and the Graphic Arts* (London: International Institute for Conservation of Historic and Artistic Works, 1972), pp. 809–815.

Laurie, Arthur P. "Restrainers and Solvents

Used in Cleaning Old Varnish from Pictures," *Technical Studies in the Field of the Fine Arts*, IV:1 (July 1935), pp. 34–41.

Lucas, A.W. "The Transfer of Easel Paintings." In *Recent Advances in Conservation* (London: Butterworths, 1963), pp. 165–168.

Majewski, Lawrence J. "On Conservation: Wall Paintings from Archaeological Finds," *Museum News*, 51:4 (December 1972), pp. 11–12.

Majewski, Lawrence J. "Results of Ageing Tests in Various In-Painting Media." In *IIC—American Group Technical Papers from 1968 through 1970* (New York: IIC–AG, 1970), pp. 75–80.

Makes, Frantisek, and Bjorn Hallstrom. *Remarks on Relining*. Stockholm: Royal Academy Art School, 1972. 44 pp., illus., bibliog.

Margaritoff, Tasso. "A New Method for Removing Successive Layers of Painting," *Studies in Conservation*, 12:4 (November 1967), pp. 140–146.

Margaritoff, Tasso. "The Removal of Successive Layers of Painting: Further Work." In *Conservation of Paintings and the Graphic Arts* (London: International Institute for Conservation of Historic and Artistic Works, 1972), pp. 815–821.

Mogford, Henry. *Handbook on the Preservation of Pictures; Containing Practical Instructions for Varnishing, Cleaning, Lining and Restoring Oil Paintings with Remarks on the Distribution of Works of Art in Houses and Galleries, and the Best Means of Preserving Them*. 14th ed., rev. London: Winsor & Newton, Ltd., n.d. 63 pp.

Mora, Paolo. "Some Observations on Mural Paintings." In *Recent Advances in Conservation* (London: Butterworths, 1963), pp. 123–124.

Murrell, Jim. "The Restoration of Portrait Miniatures." In *Conservation of Painting and the Graphic Arts* (London: International Institute for Conservation of Historic and Artistic Works, 1972), pp. 821–825.

Nicola, Guido; Gianluigi Nicola; and Roberto Arosio. "A New Facing Material," *Studies in Conservation*, 18:4 (November 1973), pp. 177–179.

Philippot, Paul, and Paolo Mora. "The Conservation of Wall Paintings." In *The Conservation of Cultural Property with Special Reference to Tropical Conditions* (Paris: UNESCO, 1968), pp. 169–189.

Plenderleith, Harold J., and Stanley Cursiter. "The Problem of Lining Adhesives for Paintings—Wax Adhesives," *Technical Studies in the Field of the Fine Arts*," III:2 (October 1934), pp. 90–113.

Rabin, Bernard. "A Contour-Fitting Mold of Paper Pulp and Methacrylate Resin for Use in Transfer," *Bulletin of the American Group—IIC*, 8:2 (1968), pp. 13–14.

Rabin, Bernard. "A Poly (vinylacetate) Heat Seal Adhesive for Lining." In *Conservation of Paintings and the Graphic Arts* (London: International Institute for Conservation of Historic and Artistic Works, 1972), pp. 631–700.

Rawlins, F. Ian G. "The Rheology of Painting," *Technical Studies in the Field of the Fine Arts*, X:2 (October 1941), pp. 59–72.

Riley, Orrin H., and Gustav A. Berger. "New Solutions for Modern Problems," *Museum News*, 51:5 (January 1973), pp. 31–36. ♦ New adhesive for consolidation of works of art.

Ruggles, Mervyn. "Transportation and Conservation of Twenty-three Mural Paintings, An Exercise in Logistics and Preservation," *Bulletin of the American Institute for Conservation of Historic and Artistic Works*, 13:2 (1973), pp. 17–29.

Ruhemann, Helmut. *The Cleaning of Paintings: Problems and Potentialities*. New York: Frederick A. Praeger, 1968. 508 pp., illus., bibliog., appendices, index. ♦ Demonstrates that clean paintings are aesthetically desirable and that cleaning has become a careful and conscientious procedure backed by scientific knowledge.

Ruhemann, Helmut. "A Record of Restoration," *Technical Studies in the Field of the Fine Arts*, III:1 (July 1934), pp. 3–15.

Sayre, Edward V. "Investigation of Italian Frescoes, Their Materials, Deterioration and Treatment." In *Application of Science in the Examination of Works of Art; Proceedings of the Seminar: June 15–19, 1970* (Boston: Museum of Fine Arts, 1973), pp. 176–181.

Shahin, A., and Otto Wachter. "Simplification of the Chlorine Dioxide Bleaching System." In *Conservation of Paintings and the Graphic Arts* (London: International Institute for Conservation of Historic and Artistic Works, 1972), pp. 955–964.

Stolow, Nathan. "Application of Science to Cleaning Methods: Solvent Action Studies on Pigmented and Unpigmented Linseed Oil Films." In *Recent Advances in Conservation* (London: Butterworths, 1963), pp. 84–88.

Stoner, J.H.; N. Indictor; and N.S. Baer. "The Effect of Metal Acetylacetonates on Fungal Attack," *Bulletin of the American Institute for Conservation of Historic and Artistic Works,* 13:2 (1973), pp. 114–121.

Stout, George L. "A Preliminary Test of Varnish Solubility," *Technical Studies in the Field of the Fine Arts,* IV:3 (January 1936), pp. 146–161.

Stout, George L. "The Restoration of a Fayum Portrait," *Technical Studies in the Field of the Fine Arts,* I:2 (October 1932), pp. 82–93.

Stout, George L. "Treatment of Blemished Paintings," *Technical Studies in the Field of the Fine Arts,* X:2 (October 1941), pp. 99–112.

Stout, George L., and Rutherford J. Gettens. "The Problem of Lining Adhesives for Paintings," *Technical Studies in the Field of the Fine Arts,* II:2 (October 1933), pp. 81–104.

Stout, George L., and Murray Pease. "A Case of Paint Cleavage," *Technical Studies in the Field of the Fine Arts,* VII:1 (July 1938), pp. 33–45.

Suhr, William. "A Built-Up Panel for Blistered Paintings on Wood," *Technical Studies in the Field of the Fine Arts,* I:1 (July 1932), pp. 29–34.

Tintori, Leonetto. "Methods Used in Italy for Detaching Murals." In *Recent Advances in Conservation* (London: Butterworths, 1963), pp. 118–122.

Tintori, Leonetto. "Scientific Assistance in the Practice of Mural Conservation in Italy." In *Application of Science in the Examination of Works of Art; Proceedings of the Seminar: June 15–19, 1970* (Boston: Museum of Fine Arts, 1973), pp. 154–163.

Tonolo, Antonio, and Clelia Giacobini. "Microbiological Changes on Frescoes." In *Recent Advances in Conservation* (London: Butterworths, 1963), pp. 62–64.

Van Ingen, W.B. "Notes on the Fungicidal Treatment of Paintings in the Canal Zone," *Technical Studies in the Field of the Fine Arts,* I:3 (January 1933), pp. 143–154.

Wales, Carroll. "Lining Torn Paintings on Aluminum Panel," *Bulletin of the American Group—IIC,* 8:2 (1968), pp. 15–17.

Watherston, M.M. "A Vacuum Table Treatment for Cupped Films on Canvas Using Chemicals and Water." In *IIC—American Group Technical Papers from 1968 through 1970* (New York: IIC-AG, 1970), pp. 121–144.

Weil, Phoebe Dent. "A New Design for Lining Stretchers," *Bulletin of The American Group—IIC,* 7:1 (October 1966), pp. 14–15.

Wolters, Christian. "Treatment of Warped Wood Panels by Plastic Deformation; Moisture Barriers; and Elastic Support." In *Recent Advances in Conservation* (London: Butterworths, 1963), pp. 163–164.

Wolters, Christian. "A Tuscan Madonna of c.1260: Technique and Conservation," *Studies in Conservation,* 2:2 (October 1955), pp. 87–96.

8

Conservation of Works of
Art on Paper

Pastels, watercolors, prints, and drawings constitute the bulk of works of art of paper, and they are a fragile yet important part of the museum's collection too frequently neglected in the conservation effort. Their treatment is a specialty and best left to the professional conservator. The care and handling of such materials, however, is the responsibility of the curator, who should be aware of their special requirements. The most useful references for the curator are Anne F. Clapp, *Curatorial Care of Works of Art on Paper* and Francis W. Dolloff, *How to Care for Works of Art on Paper.*

For the conservator, there are references in this chapter both to the materials of works of art on paper and to the techniques used in the treatment of them.

Materials

American Paper and Pulp Association.
The Dictionary of Paper, Including Pulp, Paperboard, Paper Properties and Related Papermaking Terms. 3rd ed. New York: American Paper and Pulp Association, 1965. 500 pp., bibliog.

Arad, A. "A Simple Measurement of Torsonial Rigidity of Paper," *Restaurator,* 1:2 (1969), pp. 69–77.

Arad, A. "Tear-Resistance Instrument," *Restaurator,* 1:3 (1970), pp. 165–176.

Armitage, F.K. *An Atlas of the Commoner Paper Making Fibres; An Introduction to Paper Microscopy.* London: Guildhall Publishing Co., 1957. 172 pp., illus. ◆ Includes microphotographs of fibers.

Baer, Norbert S.; N. Indictor; and A. Joel. "An Evaluation of Glues for Use in Paper Conservation." In *Conservation of Paintings and the Graphic Arts* (London: International Institute for Conservation of Historic and Artistic Works, 1972), pp. 601–612.

Browning, B.L. *Analysis of Paper.* New York: Marcel Dekker, Inc., 1969. 342 pp., illus., bibliog.

Browning, B.L. "The Nature of Paper," *Library Quarterly,* 40:1 (January 1970), pp. 18–38.

Byrne, Jerry, and Jack Weiner. *Permanence.* Appleton, Wisc.: Institute of Paper Chemistry, 1964. 115 pp. ◆ A bibliography on permanence of paper.

Hunter, Dard. *Papermaking, the History and Technique of an Ancient Craft.* 2nd ed., rev. and enl. New York: Alfred A. Knopf, 1947. 611 pp., illus., map, diagrams, bibliog.

Institute of Paper Chemistry. *Aspects of the Taiwanian Handmade Paper Industry.* Film, 21 minutes, 16 mm., color, sound (1966). ◆ Available for rent or purchase from the Institute of Paper Chemistry, P.O. Box 1048, Appleton, Wisconsin 54911.

Joel, A.; N. Indictor; J.F. Hanlan; and N.S. Baer. "The Measurement and Significance of pH in Paper Conservation," *Bulletin of the*

American Group—IIC, 12:2 (April 1972), pp. 119–125.

Stout, George L., and Minna H. Horwitz. "Experiments with Adhesives for Paper," *Technical Studies in the Field of the Fine Arts,* III:1 (July 1934), pp. 38–46.

Tamarind Lithography Workshop, Inc. *The Beauty and Longevity of an Original Print Depends Greatly on the Paper That Supports It.* Rev. ed. Los Angeles: Tamarind Lithography Workshop, 1970. 8 pp. ◆ Includes samples of some handmade papers used for printing with a description of fiber content and pH of each.

Veitch, Fletcher Pearre. *Paper-Making Materials and Their Conservation.* U.S. Department of Agriculture, Bureau of Chemistry Circular 41. Washington, D.C.: U.S. Government Printing Office, 1911. 20 pp.

Weidner, Marilyn Kemp. "Damage and Deterioration of Art on Paper Due to Ignorance and the Use of Faulty Materials," *Studies in Conservation,* 12:1 (February 1967), pp. 5–25.

Wilson, William K. "Reflections on the Stability of Paper," *Restaurator,* 1:2 (1969), pp. 79–86.

Techniques

Antreasian, Garo, with Clinton Adams. *The Tamarind Book of Lithography: Art & Technique.* Los Angeles: Tamarind Lithography Workshop, 1971. 463 pp., illus., bibliog.

Beck, Walter. "Something About Pastel Technic and Its Permanence," *Technical Studies in the Field of Fine Arts,* II:3 (January 1934), pp. 119–123.

Eppink, Norman R. *One Hundred and One Prints: The History and Techniques of Printmaking.* Norman, Okla.: University of Oklahoma Press, 1971. 273 pp., illus., bibliog.

Gross, Anthony. *Etching, Engraving, and Intaglio Printing.* New York: Oxford University Press, 1970. 172 pp., illus., bibliog.

Hind, Arthur. *Introduction to the History of Woodcut, with a Detailed Survey of Work Done in the Fifteenth Century.* 1935. Reprint. New York: Dover Publications, 1963. 2 vols. (838 pp.), illus., bibliog.

Ivins, William M., Jr. *How Prints Look: Photographs with a Commentary.* Boston: Beacon Press, c 1943, 1958. 164 pp., illus., photos, paperback.

Lyman, John. "Paper As a Ground for Oil Painting," *Technical Studies in the Field of the Fine Arts,* I:4 (April 1933), pp. 207–211.

New York (City). Metropolitan Museum of Art. *Notes on Prints.* By William M. Ivins, Jr. 1930. Reprint. Cambridge, Mass.: MIT Press, 1969. 194 pp., illus. ◆ Text of the descriptive labels accompanying a 1929 exhibition of prints.

Ross, John, and Clare Romano. *The Complete Printmaker; The Art and Technique of the Relief Print, the Intaglio Print, the Collograph, the Lithograph, the Screen Print, the Dimensional Print, Photographic Prints, Children's Prints, Collecting Prints, Print Workshop.* New York: Free Press, 1972. 306 pp., illus., bibliog.

Conservation Procedures

Banks, Paul. *Matting and Framing Documents and Art Objects on Paper.* Chicago: The Newberry Library, 1968. 6 pp., illus., bibliog., supply sources.

Beauchamp, Richard R. "A Simple Layout for Washing and Bleaching of Prints and Drawings," *Bulletin of the American Group—IIC,* 9:1 (1968) pp. 21–22.

Berger, Gustav. "A New Adhesive for the Consolidation of Paintings, Drawings and Textiles," *Bulletin of the American Group—IIC,* 11:1 (October 1970), pp. 36–38.

Boustead, William M. "The Conservation of Works of Art in Tropical and Sub-Tropical Zones." In *Recent Advances in Conservation* (London: Butterworths, 1963), pp. 73–78.

Boustead, William M. "The Surface pH Measurement and Deacidification of Prints and Drawings in Tropical Climates," *Studies in Conservation,* 9:2 (May 1964), pp. 50–58.

Clapp, Anne F. *Curatorial Care of Works of Art on Paper.* Oberlin, Ohio: Intermuseum Conservation Association, 1973. 105 pp., list of suppliers, bibliog., paperback. ◆ Includes discussions of factors potentially harmful to paper, various procedures in the care of works of art on paper, equipment and materials of the workroom and storage areas and a list of supplies and sources.

Dolloff, Francis W., and Roy L. Perkinson. *How to Care for Works of Art on Paper.* Boston: Museum of Fine Arts, 1971. 46 pp., photos, drawings, diagrams, materials source list, bibliog., paperback. ◆ Practical advice on the handling of art on paper, rules for guarding against mold, matting and framing practices and sources of materials and supplies.

Eirk, Katherine C. "An Experimental Evaluation of Accepted Methods for Removing Spots and Stains from Works of Art on Paper," *Bulletin of the American Group—IIC,* 12:2 (April 1972), pp. 82–87.

Eley, Wayne. "Framing Paper Artifacts," *Paper Conservation News,* 1:2 (July 1973), pp. 1–4.

Glaser, Mary Todd. *Framing and Preservation of Works of Art on Paper.* New York: Parke-Bernet Galleries, n.d. 4 pp., illus., bibliog.

Gunn, Maurice J. *Print Restoration and Picture Cleaning: An Illustrated Practical Guide to the Restoration of All Kinds of Prints.* London: L.U. Gill, 1911. 172 pp., illus., diagrams.

Hamelin, Bernard. *Maranyl as Fixative for Pastel.* Picture Conservation Report no. 4. Ottawa: Public Archives of Canada, 1971. 4 pp.

Harding, E.G. *The Mounting of Prints and Drawings.* London: Museums Association, 1972. 3 pp.

Honig, Mervin. "The Problem of Fungus Infestation of a Framed Pastel Portrait on Paper," *Bulletin of the American Group—IIC,* 11:2 (April 1971), pp. 129–131.

Horton, Carolyn. *Report and Recommendations on the Rescue of the Water-Damaged Books and Prints at the Corning Glass Center, Corning, New York, June 1972.* Unpublished, on deposit at the New York State Historical Association Library, Cooperstown, New York, 1972. 4 pp., supplies notes, mimeo.

International Institute for Conservation of Historic and Artistic Works. *Conservation of Paintings and the Graphic Arts.* Preprints of Contributions to the Lisbon Congress, 1972, 9–14 October, 1972. London: The Institute, 1972. 1006 pp., illus., bibliog.

Keck, Sheldon. "A Method of Cleaning Prints," *Technical Studies in the Field of the Fine Arts,* V:2 (October 1936), pp. 117–126.

King, Antoinette. "Conservation of Drawings and Prints," *Special Libraries,* 63:3 (March 1972), pp. 116–120.

King, Antoinette; Wynne Phelan; and Warren E. Falconer. "On the Choice of Paper for Lining Works of Art on Ground Wood Pulp Supports," *Studies in Conservation,* 18:4 (November 1973), pp. 171–174.

Landon, Edward. *Picture Framing: Modern Methods of Making and Finishing Picture Frames.* New York: American Artists Group, Inc., 1945. 146 pp., illus., diagrams.

Lee, H.N. "Established Methods for Examination of Paper," *Technical Studies in the Field of the Fine Arts,* IV:1 (July 1935), pp. 3–14.

Lee, H.N. "Improved Methods for the Examination of Paper," *Technical Studies in the Field of the Fine Arts,* IV:2 (October 1935), pp. 93–106.

Mates, Robert E. *Photographing Art.* Philadelphia: Chilton Books, 1966. 128 pp., illus., bibliog. ◆ Techniques used by a museum staff photographer to photograph paintings, drawings, watercolors, collages, sculpture and a variety of art objects.

Moktsova, I.P.; G.Z. Bykova; and I. Ivanova. "The Conservation Methods for Miniature Painting on Parchment." In *Conservation of Paintings and the Graphic Arts* (London: International Institute for Conservation of Historic and Artistic Works, 1972), pp. 915–919.

Plenderleith, Harold J. *The Conservation of Prints, Drawings and Manuscripts.* Oxford: Oxford University Press for The Museums Association, 1937. 66 pp., illus., bibliog., diagrams.

Ruggles, Mervyn. "Practical Application of Deacidification Treatment of Works of Art on Paper," *Bulletin of the American Group—IIC,* 11:2 (April 1971), pp. 76–84.

Tamarind Lithography Workshop, Inc. *Questions to Ask Your Framer and Answers You Should Get.* Los Angeles, Calif.:

Tamarind Lithography Workshop, 1969. 10 pp., illus.

Weidner, Marilyn Kemp. *Instructions on How to Unframe Wet Prints.* Unpublished, on deposit at the New York State Historical Association Library, Cooperstown, New York, 1972. 4 pp., materials list, mimeo.

Zigrosser, Carl, and Christa M. Gaehde. *A Guide to the Collecting and Care of Original Prints.* New York: Crown Publishers, 1965. 120 pp., illus., bibliog.

NOTE

Tamarind Lithography Workshop, 1112 North Tamarind Avenue, Los Angeles, California 90038, is a nonprofit organization devoted to the stimulation and preservation of the arts of the lithograph.

9

Conservation of Objects

All artifacts, be they iron kettles, china tea cups, or grandmother's wedding dress, are susceptible to the hazards of time, neglect, carelessness and ignorance. And, they are just as deserving of the attention of a professional conservator as are paintings or works of art on paper. The preservation of the myriad of objects which form the core of most historical society and museum collections presents some very specialized problems both for the conservator and the curator. They must work together to provide the proper care and treatment for artifact collections ranging widely in size, material and condition.

The General Reference section of this chapter provides some important references on basic care and handling of artifacts. Among those which the curator will find helpful are Per E. Guldbeck, *The Care of Historical Collections: A Conservation Handbook for the Non-Specialist,* and, Dorothy H. Dudley and Irma B. Wilkinson, et al., *Museum Registration Methods.*

The section on Materials and Technology is concerned with what the artifact is made of and how it is put together. The section on Treatment is subdivided according to the materials of which objects are made. These last two sections, which are directed primarily at the professional conservator, also include a few references which provide general information for the nonspecialist.

General Reference

"Abstracts of the Rome Conference Contributions, September 1961," *Studies in Conservation,* (November 1961), entire issue. ◆ Includes lighting, humidity control, packing, transport, methods of analysis, fungicides and insecticides, cleaning of paintings, treatment of metallic objects, consolidation of fragile objects, examination and conservation of glass, reinforcing and transfer of wood panel paintings, new picture varnishes, treatment and repair of textiles and tapestries, education and training of conservators and restorers.

Agrawal, O.P. *Short Term Course on the Care of Museum Objects, December 1, 1966 to January 31, 1967.* New Delhi: National Museum, 1967. 11 pp., mimeo.

The Conservation of Cultural Property, with Special Reference to Tropical Conditions. Museums and Monuments XI. Paris: UNESCO, 1968. 341 pp., photos, drawings, diagrams, tables, maps, formulae, appendices, bibliog., index. ◆ Articles by experts in the field on climate and microclimate, moulds, insects, conservation of glass, stone, metals, textiles, leather, wood, archival materials and paintings; recommendations on lighting, air conditioning, storage and handling. Very technical but an excellent reference on the problems of conservation in the tropics.

Dudley, Dorothy H., and Irma B. Wilkinson, et al. *Museum Registration Methods.* Rev. ed. Washington, D.C.: American Association of Museums, 1968. 294 pp., illus., forms, plans, bibliog., index. ◆ Covers aspects of storage, packing, registration, classification and inspection of art objects and includes a trial glossary for describing condition. Revised edition in progress.

Gairola, T.R. *Handbook of Chemical Conservation of Museum Objects.* Baroda, India: Department of Museology, Maharaja Sayajirao University of Baroda, 1960. 101 pp., illus., diagrams. ◆ Includes cleaning and preservation of organic materials, metals and siliceous materials.

Guldbeck, Per E. *The Care of Historical Collections: A Conservation Handbook for the Non-Specialist.* Rev. ed. Nashville, Tenn.: American Association for State and Local History, 1972. 160 pp., photos, drawings, diagrams, tables, bibliog., supply list, appendices, paperback. ◆ Provides an introduction to the problems of conservation and describes basic procedures for the care of museum collections. Includes advice on the treatment of paper, wood, leather, textiles, ceramics and related materials. Deals with the environmental aspects of conservation, documentation of artifacts, and the equipment of a conservation laboratory. Intended as a practical manual for the small historical society or museum.

Guldbeck, Per E. "Conservation and Care of Collections." AASLH Cassette Tape no. 16. Nashville, Tenn.: American Association for State and Local History, 1971. 1 cassette tape, 57 minutes. ◆ Explains what conservation is in respect to restoration and reviews details of techniques and materials used in fire protection, cleaning and repairing items, keeping records, cautions in the cleaning process, collection care and storage, and security for the collection.

Hall, E.T. "Methods of Analysis (Physical and Microchemical) Applied to Paintings and Antiquities." In *Recent Advances in Conservation* (London: Butterworths, 1963), pp. 29–32. ◆ Includes comparative merits of various types of analytical procedures: standard wet chemistry, optical emission spectrometry, x-ray fluorescent spectrometry, x-ray diffraction, electron probe microanalysis.

Keck, Sheldon. *Emergency Care of Museum Artifacts and Library Materials Affected by the Flood.* Unpublished, on deposit at the New York State Historical Association Library, Cooperstown, New York, 1972. 3 pp.

Marsh, Moreton. *The Easy Expert in Collecting and Restoring American Antiques.* 1st ed. Philadelphia: J.B. Lippincott, 1959. 176 pp., illus., bibliog., paperback. ◆ What to look for in old brasses, tool marks, dimensions, and methods of construction.

Mellan, Ibert, and Eleanor Mellan. *Removing Spots and Stains.* New York: Chemical Publishing Co., 1959. 95 pp. ◆ Available from Textile Book Service, 1447 East Second Street, Box 907, Plainfield, N.J. 17061.

Moore, Alma Chesnut. *How to Clean Everything: An Encyclopedia of What to Use and How to Use It.* Rev. ed. New York: Simon and Schuster, 1968. 224 pp., illus., bibliog.

Plenderleith, Harold J., and A.E.A. Werner. *The Conservation of Antiquities and Works of Art: Treatment, Repair and Restoration.* 2nd ed. New York: Oxford University Press, 1971. 394 pp., photos, diagrams, tables, formulae, bibliog. footnotes, index. ◆ Technical, but a basic reference in the field of conservation. Includes data on the nature of the materials in museum collections; the causes of their deterioration; and detailed information on methods of preservation, repair and restoration. Intended as a handbook for the collector, the archeologist, and the museum curator, and as a workshop guide for the technician.

Rosenquist, Anna M. "New Methods for the Consolidation of Fragile Objects." In *Recent Advances in Conservation* (London: Butterworths, 1963), pp. 140–144.

Taubes, Frederic. *Restoring and Preserving Antiques.* New York; Watson-Guptill Publications, 1969. 199 pp., illus. ◆ Includes chapters on materials, equipment, and sources of supply.

Thomson, Garry. "Preserving Precious Objects," *Science and Technology,* 74 (February 1968), pp. 33–38.

U.S. Forest Products Laboratory, Madison, Wisconsin. *List of Publications on Glues, Glued Products and Veneer.* Madison, Wisc.: U.S. Forest Products Laboratory, 1968. 32 pp.

Werner, A.E. "Consolidation of Fragile Objects." In *Recent Advances in Conservation* (London: Butterworths, 1963), pp. 125–127. ◆ Discusses consolidation of waterlogged wood, wormeaten wood, leather, ivory and bone, wall paintings, siliceous materials.

Materials and Technology

Brown, Harry P.; Alexis J. Panshin; and C.C. Forsaith. *Textbook of Wood Technology, Vol. II: Physical, Mechanical and Chemical Properties of the Commercial Woods of the United States.* New York: McGraw-Hill, 1952. 783 pp., diagrams, tables, formulae, bibliog. references, index.

Browning, B.L., ed. *The Chemistry of Wood.* New York: Interscience Publishers, 1963. 689 pp., illus., bibliog.

Caley, Earle R. *Analysis of Ancient Metals.* International Series of Monographs on Analytical Chemistry, vol. 19. New York: Macmillan Co., 1964. 176 pp., bibliog.

Caley, Earle R. "Chemical Composition of Ancient Copper Objects of South America." In *Application of Science in the Examination of Works of Art; Proceedings of the Seminar: June 15–19, 1970* (Boston: Museum of Fine Arts, 1973), pp. 53–61.

Evans, Ulick R. *Corrosion and Oxidation of Metals: First Supplementary Volume.* New York: St. Martin's Press, 1968. 488 pp., illus.

Evans, Ulick R. *The Corrosion and Oxidation of Metals; Scientific Principles and Practical Applications.* New York: St. Martin's Press, 1960. 1094 pp., illus., diagrams, bibliog.

Evans, Ulick R. *An Introduction to Metallic Corrosion.* 2nd ed. New York: St. Martin's Press, 1963. 253 pp., illus., bibliog.

Ferguson, Eugene S. *Bibliography of the History of Technology.* Cambridge, Mass.: The Society for the History of Technology, 1968. 347 pp. ◆ Available from MIT Press.

Gettens, Rutherford J. "Identification of Pigments and Inerts on Paintings and Other Museum Objects." In *Application of Science in the Examination of Works of Art; Proceedings of the Seminar: September 15–18, 1958* (Boston: Museum of Fine Arts, 1959), pp. 31–50.

Graff, John Henry. *A Color Atlas for Fiber Identification.* Appleton, Wisc.: Institute of Paper Chemistry, 1940. various pagings, illus.

Great Britain. Interservice Metallurgical Research Council. *Corrosion and Its Prevention at Bimetallic Contacts.* London: Her Majesty's Stationery Office, 1958. 9 pp., illus.

Harris, Milton. *Handbook of Textile Fibers.* 1st ed. Washington, D.C.: Harris Research Laboratories, 1954. 356 pp., illus.

Hodges, Henry. *Artifacts: An Introduction to Primitive Technology.* New York: Frederick E. Praeger, 1964. 248 pp., illus., tables, bibliog., paperback.

Hours, Madeleine, and F. Michel. "Scientific Methods in the Study of the Metallurgy of Antiquity at the Louvre." In *Application of Science in the Examination of Works of Art; Proceedings of the Seminar: June 15–19, 1970* (Boston: Museum of Fine Arts, 1973), pp. 67–72. ◆ Spectrographic analysis of an Egyptian Bronze Series.

Jane, Frank W. *The Structure of Wood.* Revised by K. Wilson and D.J.B. White. 2nd ed. London: A. & C. Black, 1970. 478 pp., illus., bibliog. ◆ Deals with gross and microscopic structure of many woods of all continents.

Kramer, Jack. *Natural Dyes, Plants and Processes.* New York: Charles Scribner's Sons, 1972. 144 pp., illus., bibliog.

Lechtman, Heather. "The Gilding of Metals in Pre-Columbian Peru." In *Application of Science in the Examination of Works of Art; Proceedings of the Seminar: June 15–19, 1970* (Boston: Museum of Fine Arts, 1973), pp. 38–52.

Lewin, Seymour Z. "A New Approach to Establishing the Authenticity of Patinas on Copper-Base Artifacts." In *Application of Science in the Examination of Works of Art; Proceedings of the Seminar: June 15–19, 1970* (Boston: Museum of Fine Arts, 1973), pp. 62–66.

Materials; A Scientific American Book. San Francisco: W.H. Freeman, 1967. 210 pp., illus., bibliog., paperback.

Moss, A.A. *The Identification of Metals.* Handbook for Museum Curators B8. London: Museums Association, 1956. 8 pp.

Norton, Frederick H. *Elements of Ceramics.*

Cambridge, Mass.: Addison Wesley Press, 1952. 246 pp., illus.

Norton, John T. "Structure of Metals and Alloys." In *Application of Science in the Examination of Works of Art: Proceedings of the Seminar: September 15–18, 1958* (Boston: Museum of Fine Arts, 1959), pp. 97–108.

O'Flaherty, Fred; William T. Roddy; and Robert M. Lollar, eds. *The Chemistry and Technology of Leather.* American Chemical Society Monograph Series No. 134. New York: Reinhold Publishing Corp., 1956–1965. 4 vols., illus., bibliog.

Panshin, Alexis J., and Carl de Zeeuw. *Textbook of Wood Technology, Vol. I: Structure, Identification, Defects and Uses of the Commercial Woods of the United States.* 3rd ed. New York: McGraw-Hill Book Co., 1970. 705 pp., photos, diagrams, tables, glossary, bibliog. notes, index.

Percy, Hubert M. *New Materials in Sculpture, Coldcasting in Metals, Glass Fibre, Polyester Resins, Vina Mold Hot Melt Compounds, Cold Cure Silastomer Flexible Moulds, Cavityless Sand Casting, Vitagel.* 2nd ed., rev. and enl. New York: Transatlantic Publishing Co., 1966. 152 pp., illus., bibliog., paperback.

Princes Risborough, Eng. Forest Products Research Laboratory. *A Handbook of Hardwoods.* London: Her Majesty's Stationery Office, 1956. 269 pp.

Princes, Risborough, Eng. Forest Products Research Laboratory. *A Handbook of Softwoods.* London: Her Majesty's Stationery Office, 1957. 73 pp.

Singer, Charles, et al., eds. *A History of Technology.* New York: Oxford University Press, 1954–1958. 5 vols., illus., maps, bibliog.

Stalker, John, and George Parker. *A Treatise of Japanning and Varnishing.* 1688. Reprint. New York: Transatlantic Arts, 1960. 84 pp., illus.

Stamm, Alfred Joaquim. *Wood and Cellulose Science.* New York: The Ronald Press Co., 1964. 549 pp., illus., bibliog.

Steinberg, Arthur. "Joining Methods on Large Bronze Statues: Some Experiments in Ancient Technology." In *Application of Science in the Examination of Works of Art; Proceedings of the Seminar: June 15–19, 1970* (Boston: Museum of Fine Arts, 1973), pp. 103–138.

Textile Institute, Manchester, England. *Identification of Textile Materials.* 6th ed., rev. and enl. Manchester: The Institute, 1970. 233 pp., illus. ◆ Distributed by Textile Book Service, 1447 East Second St., Box 907, Plainfield, New Jersey 07061.

Tiemann, Harry D. *Wood Technology: Constitution, Properties, and Uses.* 3rd ed. New York: Pitman Publishing Co., 1951. 396 pp., illus.

U.S. Forest Products Laboratory, Madison, Wisconsin. *Wood—Colors and Kinds.* Agricultural Handbook No. 101. Washington, D.C.: U.S. Department of Agriculture, Forest Service, 1956. 36 pp., illus.

U.S. Forest Products Laboratory, Madison, Wisconsin. *Wood Handbook: Basic Information on Wood as a Material of Construction with Data for Its Use in Design and Specification.* U.S. Department of Agriculture Handbook No. 72. Washington, D.C.: U.S. Government Printing Office, 1955. 528 pp., illus., maps, glossary.

Welsh, Peter C. *Tanning in the United States to 1850: A Brief History.* U.S. National Museum Bulletin #242. Washington, D.C.: Museum of History and Technology, Smithsonian Institution, 1964. 99 pp., illus., bibliog.

Conservation Treatment

Stone

Asmus, J.F.; G. Guattari; L. Lazzarini; G. Musumeci; and R.F. Wuerker. "Holography in the Conservation of Statuary," *Studies in Conservation,* 18:2 (May 1973), pp. 49–63.

Gauri, K.L.; George C. Doderer; N. Thornton Lipscomb; and Atul C. Sarma. "Reactivity of Treated and Untreated Marble Specimens in an SO_2 Atmosphere," *Studies in Conservation,* 18:1 (February 1973), pp. 25–35.

Hempel, Kenneth F.B. "Notes on the Conservation of Sculpture, Stone, Marble and Terracotta," *Studies in Conservation,* 13:1 (February 1968), pp. 34–44.

International Institute for Conservation of Historic and Artistic Works. *Conservation of Stone. Vol. I. Preprints of the Contributions to the New York Conference on Conservation of Stone and Wooden Objects, June 7–13, 1970.* 2nd ed., rev. London: The Institute, 1971. 134 pp., illus., charts, diagrams, references. ◆ Technical, a useful reference for the conservator. Includes articles on decay of stone, impregnation, removal of soluble salts, mud brick preservation, stabilization of adobe and stone and deterioration of sculptural stone.

Lazzarini, L. "The Application of Laser Radiation to the Cleaning of Statuary," *Bulletin of the American Institute for the Conservation of Historic and Artistic Works,* 13:2 (1973), pp. 39–49.

Lewin, S.Z., and N.S. Baer. "Rationale of the Barium Hydroxide—Urea Treatment of Decayed Stone," *Studies in Conservation,* 19:1 (February 1974), pp. 24–35.

Sneyers, R.V., and P.J. de Henau. "The Conservation of Stone." In *The Conservation of Cultural Property with Special Reference to Tropical Conditions* (Paris: UNESCO, 1968), pp. 209–236. ◆ Includes classification of rocks and minerals; factors causing change in stone; maintenance and conservation of stone objects; preservation, consolidation, restoration, storage, packing, and transport.

Wood

Albright, Alan B. "The Preservation of Small Water-Logged Wood Specimens with Polyethylene Glycol," *Curator,* IX:3 (September 1966), pp. 228–234.

Brommelle, Norman S., and A.E.A. Werner. "Deterioration and Treatment of Wood." In *Problems of Conservation in Museums* (Paris: Editions Eyrolles, 1969), pp. 69–118. ◆ Discusses causes of decay, treatment of insect infestation, fungal decay, consolidation, stabilization and protection of wood, restoration of furniture, movable wooden sculpture preserved indoors.

Cescinsky, Herbert. *The Gentle Art of Faking Furniture.* 1931. Reprint. New York: Dover Publications, Inc. 1967. 167 pp., index, paperback. ◆ Deals predominantly with English and Continental furniture. Stresses scholar-

ship and experience rather than "instant expert" tricks.

"Conservation, Technique and Examination of Polychromed Sculpture," *Studies in Conservation,* 15:4 (November 1970), special issue.

Deschiens, Robert, and Christine Coste. "Protection of Works of Art in Carved Wood from Attacks of Wood-Eating Insects," *Museum,* X:1 (1957), pp. 55–59.

Gorton, Edwin. "Restoration of an Eighteenth Century Writing Table," *Studies in Conservation,* 6:1 (February 1961), pp. 31–35.

Grotz, George. *The Furniture Doctor, Being Practical Information for Everybody About the Care, Repair and Refinishing of Furniture, With Easy to Follow Directions and Tricks of the Trade that Use Commonly Available Materials, All Presented with the Author's Usual Hilarious Anecdotes in the Yankee Manner and More About His Infamous Uncle George.* Garden City: Doubleday, 1962. 286 pp., illus.

Hayward, Charles H. *Furniture Repairs.* Princeton, N.J.: Van Nostrand Co., 1967. 191 pp., illus., diagrams.

Hickin, Norman E. *The Insect Factor in Wood Decay; An Account of Wood Boring Insects with Particular Reference to Timber Indoors.* 2nd ed. London: Hutchinson & Co., 1968. 344 pp., illus. map, bibliog.

Hickin, Norman E. *Wood Preservation: A Guide to the Meaning of Terms.* London: Hutchinson and Co., Ltd., 1971. 109 pp., glossary of terms, bibliog.

International Institute for Conservation of Historic and Artistic Works. *Conservation of Wooden Objects. Vol. II. Preprints of the Contributions to the New York Conference on Conservation of Stone and Wooden Objects, June 7–13, 1970.* 2nd ed. London: The Institute, 1971. 140 pp., illus., diagrams, graphs, charts, bibliog. ◆ Technical, a useful reference for the conservator. Includes articles on deterioration and its prevention, consolidation, dimensional stabilization, freeze-drying and insect damage.

Kinney, Ralph P. *The Complete Book of Furniture Repairing and Refinishing: Easy to Follow Guide with Step-by-Step Methods.*

New York: Charles Scribner's Sons, 1950. 240 pp., illus., bibliog.

Knight, Reginald A.G. *Efficiency of Adhesives for Wood.* Forest Products Research Bulletin no. 38. 2nd ed. London: Her Majesty's Stationery Office, 1959. 21 pp.

McKerrell, Hugh, and Andrew Oddy. "The Conservation of Waterlogged Wood Using Dewatering Fluids; An Evaluation," *Museums Journal,* 71:4 (March 1972), pp. 165–167.

McKerrell, Hugh; E. Roger; and A. Varsanyi. "The Acetone/Rosin Method for Conservation of Waterlogged Wood," *Studies in Conservation,* 17:3 (August 1972), pp. 111–125.

Majewski, Lawrence. "On Conservation: Preservation of Wood," *Museum News,* 51:2 (October 1972), pp. 13–14.

Martin, Mervin. *Emergency Procedures for Furniture.* Unpublished, on deposit at the New York State Historical Association Library, Cooperstown, New York, 1972. 2 pp., recipes, mimeo.

Moncrieff, A. "Review of Recent Literature on Wood," *Studies in Conservation,* 13:4 (November 1968), pp. 186–212. ◆ A bibliography from 1960–1968 on the nature and care of wood.

Mühlethaler, Bruno. *Conservation of Waterlogged Wood and Wet Leather.* Paris: Editions Eyrolles, 1973. 72 pp., illus., tables, bibliog. ◆ Deals with the present state of knowledge of the problems involved in the preservation of wood which has undergone processes of deterioration over a long time in a wet environment, more or less excluded from the air. One chapter deals with the conservation of wet leather.

Munnikendam, R.A. "Conservation of Waterlogged Wood Using Radiation Polymerization," *Studies in Conservation,* 12:2 (May 1967), pp. 70–80.

Packard, Elizabeth C.G. "The Preservation of Polychromed Wood Sculpture by the Wax Immersion and Other Methods," *Museum News,* 46:2 (October 1967), Technical Supplement no. 19. ◆ No longer available.

Pinto, Edward H., and Eva R. Pinto. *The Care of Woodwork in the Home: Cleaning, De-Worming, Repair and Surface Mainte-* *nance of Furniture and Other Movables, as Well as the Protection and Treatment of the Timber of the Structure.* London: Benn, 1955. 34 pp., illus.

Plummer, P. "Restoration of a 15th-Century English Pulpit," *Studies in Conservation,* 10:4 (November 1965), pp. 168–175.

Reed, Sally Ann. "A Fortifying Preservative for Wood and Wood Fibers," *Curator,* IX:1 (1966), pp. 41–50.

Rodd, John. *The Repair and Restoration of Furniture.* New York: Charles Scribner's Sons, 1955. 179 pp., illus.

Rosenquist, Anna M. "The Stabilizing of Wood Found in the Viking Ship of Oseberg—Part I," *Studies in Conservation,* 4:1 (February 1959), pp. 13–21.

Rosenquist, Anna M. "The Stabilizing of Wood Found in the Viking Ship of Oseberg—Part II," *Studies in Conservation,* 4:2 (May 1959), pp. 62–72.

Schaffer, E. "Consolidation of Softwood Artifacts," *Studies in Conservation,* 16:3 (August 1971), pp. 110–113.

Shell Oil Company. *Preserving the Wasa.* Film, 15 minutes, 16 mm., sound, color, free rental, (1966). ◆ Describes how the carvings and wooden objects are taken to a specially built laboratory for preservation. The hull itself must lie for years under a mist of polyethylene glycol before the work of preservation is completed. Available from Shell Film Library, 450 North Meridian Street, Indianapolis, Indiana 46204.

Stern, William L. "Limitations of Wood Anatomy in the Study of Objects of Art." In *Applications of Science in the Examination of Works of Art; Proceedings of the Seminar: September 15–18, 1958* (Boston: Museum of Fine Arts, 1959), pp. 77–86.

Stevens, W.C. "Rates of Change in the Dimensions and Moisture Contents of Wooden Panels Resulting from Changes in the Ambient Air Conditions," *Studies in Conservation,* 6:1 (February 1961), pp. 21–25.

Symposium on the Weathering of Wood, Ludwigsburg, Germany, 8–11 VI 1969. Vol. IV. Paris: ICOMOS, 1972. 259 pp., photos, diagrams, tables. ◆ Includes an extensive bibliography covering publications in French,

English, German and Polish, and a list of experts and specialized institutions. Text in French and English.

Tomashevich, G.N. "The Conservation of Water-Logged Wood." In *Problems of Conservation in Museums* (Paris: Editions Eyrolles, 1969), pp. 165–186.

U.S. Forest Products Laboratory, Madison, Wisconsin. *Forest Products Laboratory List of Publications on Wood Preservation.* Madison, Wisc.: Forest Products Laboratory, Forest Service, U.S. Department of Agriculture, 1967. 27 pp. ◆ Issued in 1959 as Forest Products Laboratory Report no. 704 under title, *List of Publications on Wood Preservation.*

Werner, A.E. "The Conservation of Leather, Wood, Bone, Ivory, and Archival Materials." In *The Conservation of Cultural Property with Special Reference to Tropical Conditions* (Paris: UNESCO, 1968), pp. 265–290.

Metal

Burns, Robert M., and William W. Bradley. *Protective Coatings for Metals.* 3rd ed. New York: Reinhold Publishing Corp., 1967. 735 pp., illus., diagrams, bibliog. footnotes. ◆ American Chemical Society Monograph Series.

Caley, Earle R. "Coatings and Incrustations on Lead Objects from the Agora and the Method Used for Their Removal," *Studies in Conservation,* 2:2 (October 1955), pp. 49–54.

Cesareo, R.; S. Sciuti; and M. Marabelli. "Non-Destructive Analysis of Ancient Bronzes," *Studies in Conservation,* 18:2 (May 1973), pp. 64–80.

Cushing, Daniel. "Corrosion and Corrosion Products of Ancient Non-Ferrous Metals." In *Application of Science in the Examination of Works of Art; Proceedings of the Seminar: September 15–18, 1958* (Boston: Museum of Fine Arts, 1959), pp. 109–138.

Evans, Ulick R. *Metallic Corrosion, Passivity and Protection.* London: E. Arnold & Co., 1946. 863 pp., illus., diagrams, bibliog. footnotes.

Fales, Mrs. Dean A., Jr. "The Care of Antique Silver," *History News,* 22:2 (February 1967), Technical Leaflet no. 40 (new series).

Gettens, Rutherford J. "Mineral Alteration Products on Ancient Metal Objects." In *Recent Advances in Conservation* (London: Butterworths, 1963), pp. 89–92.

Gordus, Adon A. "Neutron Activation Analysis of Streaks from Coins and Metallic Works of Art." In *Application of Science in the Examination of Works of Art; Proceedings of the Seminar: June 15–19, 1970* (Boston: Museum of Fine Arts, 1973), pp. 9–17.

Great Britain. Interservice Metallurgical Research Council. *Corrosion of Metals by Vapours from Organic Materials: A Survey.* By Vera E. Rance and H.G. Cole. London: Her Majesty's Stationery Office, 1958. 24 pp.

Hamelin, Bernard. *Metals and Alloys: Their Degradation and Conservation.* Ottawa: Public Archives of Canada, 1971. 12 pp., bibliog.

Janes, Patricia A. "Preserving Bronze Antiquities," *Curator,* 8:1 (1965), pp. 72–77.

Jedrzejewska, Hanna. "The Conservation of Ancient Bronzes," *Studies in Conservation,* 9:1 (February 1964), pp. 23–31. ◆ Includes cleaning, protective treatments, examination and recording.

Jedrzejewska, Hanna. "Sampling Precautions in the Analysis of Metallic Antiquities," *Studies in Conservation,* 7:1 (February 1962), pp. 27–32.

Jedrzejewska, Hanna. "Some New Experiments in the Conservation of Ancient Bronzes." In *Recent Advances in Conservation* (London: Butterworths, 1963), pp. 135–139.

Keyser, Barbara. "A Technical Study of Two Late Chou Bronze Chiens," *Bulletin of the American Institute for Conservation of Historic and Artistic Works,* 13:2 (1973), pp. 50–64.

Lemmer, Geoffrey M. "The Cleaning and Protective Coating of Ferrous Metals," *Bulletin of the American Group—IIC,* 12:2 (April 1972), pp. 97–109.

Majewski, Lawrence. "On Conservation: Silver," *Museum News,* 51:9 (April 1973), pp. 10–11.

Meyers, Pieter, and Edward V. Sayre. "The Determination of Trace Elements in Ancient Silver Objects by Thermal Neutron Activation

Analysis," *Bulletin of the American Group—IIC,* 11:2 (April 1971), pp. 29–33.

Moss, A.A. *Electrotyping.* Handbook for Museum Curators B5. London: Museums Association, 1956. 12 pp.

Myers, Ward R. "Metallurgical Problems in Identifying Objects of Silver and Copper Alloys," *Bulletin of the American Group—IIC,* 10:2 (April 1970), pp. 15–24.

Oddy, W.A., and M.J. Hughes. "The Stabilization of 'Active' Bronze and Iron Antiquities by the Use of Sodium Sesquicarbonate," *Studies in Conservation,* 15:3 (August 1970), pp. 183–189.

Organ, Robert M. "Aspects of Bronze Patina and Its Treatment," *Studies in Conservation,* 8:1 (February 1963), pp. 1–9.

Organ, Robert M. "Conservation of Iron Objects," *Historical Archaeology,* Vol. I (1967), pp. 52–53.

Organ, Robert M. "The Consolidation of Fragile Metallic Objects." In *Recent Advances in Conservation* (London: Butterworths, 1963), pp. 128–134.

Organ, Robert M. "The Examination and Treatment of Bronze Antiquities." In *Recent Advances in Conservation* (London: Butterworths, 1963), pp. 104–110.

Organ, Robert M. "Examination of the Ardagh Chalice—A Case History." In *Application of Science in the Examination of Works of Art; Proceedings of the Seminar: June 15–19, 1970* (Boston: Museum of Fine Arts, 1973), pp. 238–271.

Organ, Robert M. "Spot-Tests for Application Directly to Metals," *Bulletin of the American Group—IIC,* 10:1 (October 1969), pp. 17–19. ◆ Simple tests suitable for direct application to the surface of metal museum objects with a view to establishing the nature of the metal without defacing it. Suitable for the small museum.

Panseri, C., and M. Leoni. "Advanced Methods for the Metallurgical Examination of Archaeological Metal Objects." In *Recent Advances in Conservation* (London: Butterworths, 1963), pp. 101–103.

Pearson, C. "The Preservation of Iron Cannon after 200 Years Under the Sea," *Studies in Conservation,* 17:3 (August 1972), pp. 91–110. ◆ Treatments used to stabilize iron cannon and carriage remains: electrolytic reduction and treatment in an activated molten caustic soda bath.

Pelikan, J.B. "Conservation of Iron with Tannin," *Studies in Conservation,* 11:3 (August 1966), pp. 109–114.

Pelikan, J.B. "The Use of Polyphosphate Complexes in the Conservation of Iron and Steel Objects," *Studies in Conservation,* 9:2 (May 1964), pp. 59–66.

Peterson, Harold L. "Conservation of Metals," *History News,* 23:2 (February 1968), Technical Leaflet no. 10. ◆ Describes basic conservation measures for iron, brass, bronze, copper, german silver, pewter, silver and gold.

Plenderleith, Harold J., and Robert M. Organ. "The Decay and Conservation of Museum Objects of Tin," *Studies in Conservation,* 1:2 (June 1953), pp. 63–72.

Plenderleith, Harold J., and G. Toracca. "The Conservation of Metals in the Tropics." In *The Conservation of Cultural Property with Special Reference to Tropical Conditions* (Paris: UNESCO, 1968), pp. 237–250. ◆ Includes electrochemical reactions of metallic objects; electrochemical, electrolytic and mechanical cleaning; impregnation; special methods in treating silver, copper, iron, and lead.

Preston, R. St. John. *Bituminous Coatings for the Protection of Iron and Steel Against Corrosion, With Special Reference to Tar Coatings and Marine Corrosion.* Department of Scientific and Industrial Research. Chemistry Research Special Report No. 5. London: Her Majesty's Stationery Office, 1946. 38 pp., references.

Rees-Jones, Stephen G. "Some Aspects of Conservation of Iron Objects from the Sea," *Studies in Conservation,* 17:1 (February 1972), pp. 39–43. ◆ A description of the methods used to conserve iron objects from the wreck of the Spanish Galleas Girona which sank in 1588 off the coast of Ireland. Reference to instability of cast iron after prolonged immersion in sea water.

Smith, Cyril Stanley. "An Examination of the Arsenic Rich Coating on a Bronze Bull from Horoztepe." In *Application of Science in the Examination of Works of Art; Proceedings of* the Seminar: June 15–19, 1970 (Boston: Museum of Fine Arts, 1973), pp. 96–102.

Stambolov, Todor. *The Corrosion and Conservation of Metallic Antiquities and Works of Art: A Preliminary Survey.* Amsterdam: Central Research Laboratory for Objects of Art and Science, n.d. 196 pp., illus.

Stambolov, Todor. "Removal of Corrosion on an 18th Century Silver Bowl," *Studies in Conservation,* 11:1 (February 1966), pp. 37–44.

Ternbach, Joseph. "Restoration of Bronzes, Ancient and Modern," *Bulletin of the American Group—IIC,* 12:2 (April 1972), pp. 110–116.

Western, A.C. "The Conservation of Excavated Iron Objects," *Studies in Conservation,* 17:2 (May 1972), pp. 83–87.

Wever, Gayle. "Mechanical Cleaning of Two Composite Objects," *Curator,* XII:3 (September 1969), pp. 194–200.

Whitmore, Florence E., and William J. Young. "Application of the Laser Microprobe and Electron Microprobe in the Analysis of Platiniridium Inclusions of Gold." In *Application of Science in the Examination of Works of Art; Proceedings of the Seminar: June 15–19, 1970* (Boston: Museum of Fine Arts, 1973), pp. 88–95.

Glass and Ceramics

Bimson, M. "The Examination of Ceramics by X-Ray Powder Diffraction," *Studies in Conservation,* 14:2 (May 1969), pp. 83–89.

Brill, Robert H., and Sheldon Moll. "The Electron-Beam Probe Microanalysis of Ancient Glass." In *Recent Advances in Conservation* (London: Butterworths, 1963), pp. 145–151.

Caley, Earle R. *Analysis of Ancient Glasses, 1790–1957: A Comprehensive and Critical Survey.* Corning Museum of Glass Monographs, Vol. I. Corning, N.Y.: Corning Museum of Glass, 1962. 118 pp., tables, bibliog. footnotes.

Errett, Raymond. "The Repair and Restoration of Glass Objects," *Bulletin of the American Group—IIC,* 12:2 (April 1972), pp. 48–49.

Fink, Colin. "Incrustations on Porous Pottery: A New Method of Cleaning Without Loss of Pigment," *Technical Studies in the Field of the Fine Arts,* II:2 (October 1933), pp. 59–61.

Fleming, Stuart J. "Authenticity Testing of Art Ceramics by the Thermoluminescence Method—Some Important Examples." In *Application of Science in the Examination of Works of Art; Proceedings of the Seminar: June 15–19, 1970* (Boston: Museum of Fine Arts, 1973), pp. 206–213.

Gedye, I. "Pottery and Glass." In *The Conservation of Cultural Property with Special Reference to Tropical Conditions* (Paris: UNESCO, 1968), pp. 109–114. ◆ On pottery: washing, marking, mending, painting. On glass: preservation, joining and filling gaps. Includes bibliography.

Gibson, Bethune M. "Methods of Removing White and Black Deposits from Ancient Pottery," *Studies in Conservation,* 16:1 (February 1971), pp. 18–21. ◆ Method for the removal of certain black and white deposits found on ancient South Italian and Etruscan pottery.

Klein, William Karl. *Repairing and Restoring China and Glass: The Klein Method.* 1st ed. New York: Harper & Row, 1962. 291 pp., illus.

Larney, J. "Ceramic Restoration in the Victoria and Albert Museum," *Studies in Conservation,* 16:2 (May 1971), pp. 69–82. ◆ The process are discussed in the order in which they would normally occur, covering the breaking down of old repairs, bonding and the adhesives used, through to the final retouching of the object.

Lowe, W. "The Conservation of Stained Glass," *Studies in Conservation,* 5:4 (November 1960), pp. 139–149. ◆ See also comment in *Journal of the Society of Master Glass-Painters,* 13:4 (1962–1963), pp. 582–584.

Moncrieff, Anne. "Lamination of Stained Glass at Cologne," *IIC News,* supplement to *Studies in Conservation,* 19:1 (February 1974), pp. 3–6.

Norton, Fred H. "Clay Deposits as a Means of Identifying Pottery." In *Application of Science in the Examination of Works of Art; Proceedings of the Seminar: September 15–18, 1958* (Boston: Museum of Fine Arts, 1959), pp. 139–144.

Parsons, Claudia S.M., and F.H. Curl. *China Mending and Restoration.* London: Faber and Faber, 1963. 435 pp., illus., bibliog. ♦ Discusses rivetting, dowelling, casting, overpainting and other techniques of china and glass repair. Stresses the importance of confining restoration to damaged areas and warns against excessive overpainting.

St. Gaudens, Paul, and Arthur R. Jackson. *How to Mend China and Bric-a-Brac, As a Hobby, As a Business.* Boston: Charles T. Branford Co., 1953. 131 pp., illus.

Sayre, E.V. "Studies of Ancient Ceramic Objects by Means of Neutron Bombardment and Emission Spectroscopy." In *Application of Science in the Examination of Works of Art; Proceedings of the Seminar: September 15–18, 1958* (Boston: Museum of Fine Arts, 1959), pp. 153–180.

Werner, A.E. "The Care of Glass in Museums," *Museum News,* 44:10 (June 1966), Technical Supplement no. 13.

Wihr, Rolf. "Possibilities of Restoration and Reproduction of Ancient Glass by the Use of Pourable Synthetic Resins," *Bulletin of the American Group—IIC,* 11:1 (October 1970), pp. 17–25.

Wihr, Rolf. "Repair and Reproduction of Ancient Glass." In *Recent Advances in Conservation* (London: Butterworths, 1963), pp. 152–155.

Wilson, Shari. "Restoring Pottery," *Curator,* XI:2 (June 1968), pp. 154–164.

Wolff, E.G. "Pottery Restoration," *Curator,* III:1 (1960), pp. 75–87. ♦ A practical working procedure, particularly for archeologists who are trying to conjecture the shape of a pot from a limited number of sherds.

Leather

Banks, Paul N. *Treating Leather Bookbinding.* Rev. ed. Chicago: Newberry Library, 1967. 4 pp., photocopy.

Belaya, I.K. "Methods of Strengthening the Damaged Leather of Old Bindings," *Restaurator,* 1:2 (1969), pp. 93–104.

Belaya, I.K. "Selecting and Testing Adhesives for the Restoration of Skinbindings and Parchments," *Restaurator,* 1:4 (1970), pp. 221–231.

Gansser, A. "The Early History of Tanning," *CIBA Review,* 81 (August 1950), entire issue. ♦ Includes principles of tanning, dressing of raw hides, tanning materials and tools, primitive methods of tanning, the coloring of leather, basic types of leather, preservation of skins and leathers.

Guldbeck, Per E. "Leather: Its Understanding and Care," *History News,* 24:4 (April 1969), Technical Leaflet no. 1. ♦ Provides a summary of the various ways of preparing skins and gives advice on the basic principles of leather care and treatment.

Middleton, Bernard C. *The Restoration of Leather Bindings.* Chicago: American Library Association, Library Technology Program, 1972. 201 pp., illus., bibliog.

Mühlethaler, Bruno. *Conservation of Waterlogged Wood and Wet Leather.* Paris: Editions Eyrolles, 1973. 72 pp., illus., tables, bibliog.

Nopitsch, M. "Micro-Organic Attack on Textiles and Leather," *CIBA Review,* 100 (October 1953), pp. 3582–3614.

Rogers, J.S., and C.W. Beebe. *Leather Bookbindings: How to Preserve Them.* U.S.D.A. Leaflet no. 398. Washington, D.C.: U.S. Government Printing Office, 1956. 8 pp., illus.

Stambolov, Todor. *Manufacture, Deterioration and Preservation of Leather: A Literature Survey of Theoretical Aspects and Ancient Techniques.* Amsterdam: ICOM Committee for Conservation, 1969. 98 pp., references. ♦ Unpublished report available from the International Centre for the Study of the Preservation and the Restoration of Cultural Property, 13 Via di San Michele, 00153, Rome, Italy.

Velich, R. "The Repair and Cleaning of an Old Painted Buffalo Robe," *Curator,* VIII:4 (December 1965), pp. 319–324.

Waterer, John W. *Guide to Conservation and Restoration of Objects Made Wholly Or in Part of Leather.* New York: Drake Publishers, 1972. 60 pp., glossary, bibliog. ♦ Gives brief but fundamental instructions on various aspects of leather conservation and restoration. Indicates specific procedures, materials and recipes. Includes deterioration of untanned hide and skin.

Waterer, John W. "A Novel Method for the Conservation of Fragile Leather," *Studies in Conservation,* 17:3 (August 1972), pp. 126–130.

Werner, A.E. "The Conservation of Leather, Wood, Bone, Ivory, and Archival Materials." In *The Conservation of Cultural Property with Special Reference to Tropical Conditions* (Paris: UNESCO, 1968), pp. 265–290. ◆ On leather: mould growth, insect attack, brittleness. On wood: adhesives and consolidants, protective coatings, waterlogged wood, painted wood. On bone and ivory: consolidation in the field, treatment in the laboratory. On archival material: control of insects, mould growth, methods of treatment. Includes bibliography.

Bone and Ivory

Baer, N.S.; B. Appelbaum; and N. Indictor. "The Effect of Long-Term Heating on Ivory," *Bulletin of the American Group—IIC,* 12:1 (1971), pp. 55–59.

Baer, N.S., et al. "Technical Investigations of Ivory: A Preliminary Report." In *IIC-American Group Technical Papers from 1968 through 1970* (New York: IIC-AG, 1970), pp. 73–74.

Baer, N.S.; N. Indictor; J.H. Frantz; and B. Appelbaum. "The Effect of High Temperature on Ivory," *Studies in Conservation,* 16:1 (February 1971), pp. 1–8.

Baer, N.S.; and Lawrence J. Majewski. "Ivory and Related Materials in Art and Archaeology: An Annotated Bibliography, Section A, Conservation and Scientific Investigation," *Art and Archaeology Technical Abstracts,* 8:2 (December 1970), pp. 229–272, supplement.

Majewski, Lawrence J. "On Conservation: Ivory and Bone," *Museum News,* 51:8 (March 1973), pp. 10–11.

Werner, A.E. "The Conservation of Leather, Wood, Bone, Ivory, and Archival Materials." In *The Conservation of Cultural Property With Special Reference to Tropical Conditions* (Paris: UNESCO, 1968), pp. 265–290. ◆ On leather: mould growth, insect attack, brittleness. On wood: adhesives and consolidants,

protective coatings, waterlogged wood, painted wood. On bone and ivory: consolidation in the field, treatment in the laboratory. On archival material: control of insects, mould growth, practical methods of treatment. Includes bibliography.

Textiles

Beecher, E.R. "The Conservation of Textiles." In *The Conservation of Cultural Property with Special Reference to Tropical Conditions* (Paris: UNESCO, 1968), pp. 251–264. ◆ Includes identification of textiles, cleaning, sterilizing and mothproofing, protection of textiles on display, reinforcing textiles.

Beecher, E.R. "Reinforcing Weakened Textiles with Synthetic-Fibre Net." In *Recent Advances in Conservation* (London: Butterworths, 1963), pp. 195–196.

Bellinger, Louisa. "Basic Habits of Textile Fibres." *Recent Advances in Conservation* (London: Butterworths, 1963), pp. 192–194.

Berger, Gustav. "A New Adhesive for the Consolidation of Paintings, Drawings and Textiles," *Bulletin of the American Group— IIC,* 11:1 (October 1970), pp. 36–38.

Columbus, Joseph V. "Tapestry Restoration in the National Gallery," *Bulletin of the American Institute for Conservation of Historic and Artistic Works,* 13:2 (1973), pp. 65–76.

Columbus, Joseph V. "Washing Techniques Used at the Textile Museums," *Bulletin of the American Group—IIC,* 7:2 (1967), pp. 14–16.

Conference on the Conservation of Textiles, Delft, 1964. Collected Preprints. 2nd ed. London: International Institute for Conservation, 1964. 153 pp., illus., charts, tables. ◆ Includes biodeterioration of textiles and its prevention; cleaning, repair and renovation; color fading and fixation; education of restorers.

Delacorte, Malcolm; Edward V. Sayre; and Norman Indictor. "Lubrication of Deteriorated Wool," *Studies in Conservation,* 16:1 (February 1971), pp. 9–17.

Fikioris, Margaret A. *First Steps to be Taken for Emergency Treatment of Textiles.* Unpublished, on deposit at the New York State Historical Association Library, Cooperstown, New York, 1972. 2 pp.

Fikioris, Margaret A. "A Model for Textile Storage," *Museum News,* 52:3 (November 1973), pp. 34–41.

Finch, Karen. "Laboratory and Studio Notes—Conservation of a Dress," *Studies in Conservation,* 8:3 (August 1963), pp. 106–111.

Fulton, George P. *Applied Science for Drycleaners.* Silver Spring, Md.: National Institute of Drycleaning, 1951. 309 pp., illus.

Geijer, Agnes. "The Conservation of Textiles," *Museum,* XIV:1 (1961), pp. 161–168.

Geijer, Agnes. "Preservation of Textile Objects." In *Recent Advances in Conservation* (London: Butterworths, 1963), pp. 185–189.

Geijer, Agnes. "Treatment and Repair of Textiles and Tapestries," *Studies in Conservation,* 6:4 (November 1961), pp. 144–145.

Giffen, Jane C. "Care of Textiles and Costumes: Cleaning and Storage Techniques," *History News,* 25:12 (December 1970), Technical Leaflet no. 2 (new series).

Glover, Jean M. *Textiles: Their Care and Protection in Museums.* Museums Association Information Sheet No. 18. London: Museums Association, 1973. 9 pp., bibliog. ◆ Discusses light, atmospheric pollution, temperature, humidity, insects, handling, storage, display, cleaning and repair.

Greene, Francina S. "The Cleaning and Mounting of a Large Wool Tapestry," *Studies in Conservation,* 2:1 (March 1955), pp. 1–16.

Greene, Francina S. "The Conservation of an Historic Robe," *Museum News,* 43:1 (September 1964), pp. 26–32. ◆ Specific details on the cleaning and repair of an 18th century robe.

Hearle, J.W.S., and R.H. Peters. *Moisture in Textiles.* London: Butterworths and the Textile Institute, 1960. 203 pp., illus., bibliog.

Hofenk-DeGraaff, Judith H. "The Constitution of Detergents in Connection with the Cleaning of Ancient Textiles," *Studies in Conservation,* 13:3 (August 1968), pp. 122–141. ◆ Includes various aspects of washing, constitution of detergents and their function, and a list of trade names.

Keck, Caroline K. "Care of Textiles and Costumes: Adaptive Techniques for Basic Maintenance," *History News,* 29:2 (February 1974), Technical Leaflet no. 71 (new series). ◆ Gives practical advice to the museum curator on the proper storage and maintenance of various types of textiles.

Konrad, A.J., and Kathryn Scott. "Restoration of a Painted Banner." In *IIC-American Group Technical Papers from 1968 through 1970* (New York: IIC-AG, 1970), pp. 151–156.

Landi, Sheila. "Notes on the Use of a Vacuum Hot-Table for Textiles," *Studies in Conservation,* 18:4 (November 1973), pp. 167–171.

Landi, Sheila. "Three Examples of Textile Conservation in the Victoria and Albert Museum," *Studies in Conservation,* 11:3 (August 1966), pp. 143–159.

Leene, Jentina E. "Restoration and Preservation of Ancient Textiles, and Natural Science." In *Recent Advances in Conservation* (London: Butterworths, 1963), pp. 190–191.

Leene, Jentina E., ed. *Textile Conservation.* Washington, D.C.: Smithsonian Institution, 1972. 275 pp., illus., diagrams, bibliog. footnotes, index. ◆ Technical, aimed primarily at conservators. Articles on characteristics of textiles and dyestuffs, principles of cleaning and storage and techniques of restoration of flat textiles, uniforms, dresses, lace, feather work, beadwork and leather.

Lehmann, Detlef. "Conservation of Textiles at the West Berlin State Museums," *Studies in Conservation,* 9:1 (February 1964), pp. 9–22. ◆ Identification, cleaning, repair, reinforcement, mothproofing, synthetic resins.

McHugh, Maureen C. "Conservation Challenge: A Seventeenth Century Linen Handerchief," *Museum News,* 46:6 (February 1968), Technical Supplement no. 21.

Majewski, Lawrence J. "On Conservation: Textiles," *Museum News,* 51:6 (January 1973), pp. 10–11.

Martin, Albert R. "Drycleaning Museum Textiles," *Bulletin of the American Group—IIC,* 7:2 (1967), pp. 9–13.

Moss, A.J.E. *Stain Removal; The Technique of Spotting; A Manual for Instructors and Students of Dry-Cleaning.* London: Published for "Power Laundry" by Trader Publishing Co., distributed by Iliffe, 1950. 179 pp., illus.

Moss, A.J.E. *Textiles and Fabrics, Their Care and Preservation.* 1st American ed. New York: Chemical Publishing Co., 1961. 560 pp., illus. ◆ Modern, non-museum techniques for those who clean and renovate textiles, furs, carpets, etc.

Myers, George H. "Rugs: Preservation, Display and Storage," *Museum News,* 43:6 (February 1965), Technical Supplement no. 6.

Nopitsch, M. "Micro-Organic Attack on Textiles and Leather," *CIBA Review,* 100 (October 1953), pp. 3582–3614. ◆ Articles include: "The Discovery of Microbes"; "Microbial Deterioration of Wool and Other Animal Fibers"; "Microbial Damage to Vegetable Fibers"; "Decay of Fishing Nets Through Microbiological Action"; "Micro-organic Attack on Leather"; "Identification of Microbial Damage"; "Preventive Treatments for Textiles and Leather."

Padfield, Tim, and Sheila Landi. "The Light-Fastness of the Natural Dyes," *Studies in Conservation,* 11:4 (November 1966), pp. 181–196.

Pow, Constance V. "The Conservation of Tapestries for Museum Display," *Studies in Conservation,* 15:2 (May 1970), pp. 134–153.

Preservation Department, Textile Museum. "Principles of Practical Cleaning for Old and Fragile Textiles," *Museum News,* 43:6 (February 1965), Technical Supplement no. 6.

Randlett, Judson C., and William J. Nicklaw. *Spotting.* Silver Spring, Md.: Institute of Dry Cleaning, 1956. 250 pp., illus. ◆ Very important manual on removing stains from textiles.

Reeves, Pat. "Alternate Methods of Hanging Tapestries," *Bulletin of the American Institute for Conservation of Historic and Artistic Works,* 13:2 (1973), pp. 86–98.

Rice, James W. "Drycleaning Versus Wetcleaning for Treating Textile Artifacts," *Bulletin of the American Group—IIC,* 12:2 (April 1972), pp. 50–55.

Rice, James W. "An Heirloom Patchwork Quilt and Its Conservation Problems," *Studies in Conservation,* 11:1 (February 1966), pp. 1–7.

Rice, James W. "The Lincoln Assassination Garments: A Case Study in Cleaning," *Museum News,* 47:6 (February 1969), Technical Supplement.

Schwarz, Edward R. "The Inside Story of Textiles." In *Application of Science in the Examination of Works of Art; Proceedings of the Seminar: September 15–18, 1958* (Boston: Museum of Fine Arts, 1959), pp. 145–152.

Sieders, R.; J.W.H. Uytenhogaart; and J.E. Leene. "The Restoration and Preservation of Old Fabrics," *Studies in Conservation,* 2:4 (October 1956), pp. 161–169.

Smith, James B., Jr. "Conservation of the Regimental Unit Color—The U.S. Treasury Guard," *Studies in Conservation,* 14:3 (August 1969), pp. 119–125. ◆ Conservation of a 107 year old American flag with painted heraldic device.

U.S. Agricultural Research Service. Consumer and Food Economic Research Division. *Removing Stains from Fabrics, Home Methods.* Home and Garden Bulletin no. 62. Rev. Washington, D.C.: U.S. Department of Agriculture, 1968. 32 pp., photos, drawings, index, paperback. ◆ A good primer for those with no specialized training.

Van Beek, H.C.A., and P.M. Heertjes. "Fading by Light of Organic Dyes on Textiles and Other Materials," *Studies in Conservation,* 11:3 (August 1966), pp. 123–132.

NOTES AND PERIODICALS

International Fabricare Institute, 8001 Georgia Avenue, Silver Springs, Maryland 20910. The International Fabricare Institute (formerly the National Institute of Drycleaning and the American Institute of Laundering) provides information and bulletin services on processes and fabrics. It offers vocational school courses in several areas including leather processing, spot removal, silk finishing and wool finishing.

It maintains laboratories at Silver Springs, Maryland and Glendale, California to analyze damaged garments sent by members.

Textile Museum Journal. 1962, annual, membership. The Textile Museum, 2320 S Street, N.W., Washington, D.C. 20008. ◆ Formerly *Workshop Notes.*

Archeological Materials

Barghoorn, E.S. "Collecting and Preserving Botanical Materials of Archaeological Interest," *American Antiquity*, 9:3 (1944), pp. 289–294.

Caley, Earle R. "Coatings and Incrustations on Lead Objects from the Agora and the Method Used for Their Removal," *Studies in Conservation*, 2:2 (October 1955), pp. 49–54.

Conference on Underwater Archaeology, St. Paul, 1963. *Diving Into the Past: Theories, Techniques, and Application of Underwater Archaeology.* The Proceedings of a Conference on Underwater Archaeology, sponsored by the Minnesota Historical Society, St. Paul, April 26–27, 1963. Edited by June D. Holmquist and Ardis H. Wheeler. St. Paul: Minnesota Historical Society, 1964. 111 pp., photos, drawings, diagrams, bibliog., index.

Dowman, Elizabeth A. *Conservation in Field Archaeology.* London: Methuen, 1970. 170 pp., illus., bibliog., index. ◆ Describes in simple form treatments which may safely be carried out on archeological finds in the field.

Majewski, Lawrence J. "The Conservation of Archaeological Materials at Sardis, Turkey," *Bulletin of the American Institute for Conservation of Historic and Artistic Works*, 13:2 (1973), pp. 99–104.

Majewski, Lawrence J. "On Conservation: Archaeological Materials," *Museum News*, 51:1 (September 1972), p. 8.

Majewski, Lawrence J. "On Conservation: Archaeological Sites," *Museum News*, 51:3 (November 1972), pp. 11–12.

Pearson, C. "The Preservation of Iron Cannon after 200 Years Under the Sea," *Studies in Conservation*, 17:3 (August 1972), pp. 91–110.

Peterson, Mendel. *History Under the Sea: A Manual for Underwater Exploration.* Rev. ed. Washington, D.C.: Smithsonian Institution Press, 1969. 208 pp., illus., maps, bibliog. ◆ A handbook on underwater archeology, with a section devoted to the problems and solutions of conserving materials from a marine environment.

Rees-Jones, S.G. "Some Aspects of Conservation of Iron Objects from the Sea," *Studies in Conservation*, 17:1 (February 1972), pp. 39–43.

Rosenquist, Anna. "The Stabilizing of Wood Found in the Viking Ship of Oseberg—Part I," *Studies in Conservation*, 4:1 (February 1959), pp. 13–21.

Rosenquist, Anna M. "The Stabilizing of Wood Found in the Viking Ship of Oseberg—Part II," *Studies in Conservation*, 4:2 (May 1959), pp. 62–72.

Seborg, Ray M., and Robert B. Inverarity. "The Conservation of 200-Year-Old Water-Logged Boats with Polyethylene Glycol," *Studies in Conservation*, 7:4 (November 1962), pp. 111–120.

Smith, J.B., and J.P. Ellis. "The Preservation of Underwater Archaeological Specimens in Plastic," *Curator*, VI:1 (1963), pp. 32–36.

Western, A.C. "The Conservation of Excavated Iron Objects," *Studies in Conservation*, 17:2 (May 1972), pp. 83–87.

Wheeler, Sir Robert E.M. *Archaeology from the Earth.* Baltimore: Penguin Books, Inc., 1961. 252 pp., illus., maps, tables, bibliog., paperback.

Other Objects

Berner, Alfred; J.H. van der Meer; and G. Thibault. *Preservation and Restoration of Musical Instruments: Provisional Recommendations.* Sponsored by ICOM International Committee on Museums and Collections. London: Evelyn, Adams & MacKay, 1967. 77 pp., illus., bibliog. ◆ Deals only with European instruments.

Clark, Joe W. *Survey of Totem Poles in S.E. Alaska and Recommendations for Their Preservation or Recovery.* Madison, Wisc.: Forest Products Laboratory, U.S. Department of Agriculture, 1970. 21 pp., illus., bibliog.

Drost, William E. "Caring for Clocks," *History News*, 23:9 (September 1968), Technical Leaflet no. 47 (new series).

Fall, Frieda Kay. "Enamelled Objects: Care and Preservation," *Museum News*, 45:10 (June 1967), Technical Supplement no. 18.

Givens, Larry. *Rebuilding the Player Piano.*

Vestal, N.Y.: Vestal Press, 1963. 164 pp., illus.

Gyermeck, Stephen A. "Conservation of Ethnological Materials," *Museum News*, 43:2 (October 1964), Technical Supplement no. 4.

Hayes, P.A. "Storage Racks for Service Swords," *Museums Journal*, 71:1 (June 1971), pp. 29–30.

Henson, William. "Restoration of Modern Machinery," *Museum News*, 49:10 (June 1971), pp. 13–17.

Johnston, Waldo C.M. "Mystic Seaport's Ship Restoration Program," *The Log of Mystic Seaport*, 19:3 (Autumn 1967), pp. 66–81.

Majewski, Lawrence. "On Conservation: Ethnographic Collections," *Museum News*, 51:7 (February 1973), pp. 8–10.

Murrell, Vernon J. "Some Aspects of the Conservation of Wax Models," *Studies in Conservation*, 16:3 (August 1971), pp. 95–109. ◆ A full account of the restoration work carried out on an allegorical tableau by Gaetano Zumbo and on two 17th century ecclesiastical dolls.

Rabin, Bernard. *Emergency Procedures for Musical Instruments.* Unpublished, on deposit at the New York State Historical Association Library, Cooperstown, New York, 1966. 1 p.

Reid, David (of Robertland), and Anne Ross.

"The Conservation of Non-Metallic Seals," *Studies in Conservation*, 15:1 (February 1970), pp. 51–62. ◆ Usual causes and forms of damage together with various methods of treatment, composition and manufacture; cleaning and repair; shellac and other thermoplastic compounds; methods of packing and storage.

Tahk, Christopher. "An X-Ray Look into Wood Movements," *Bulletin of the National Association of Watch and Clock Collectors, Inc.*, XV:11 (whole no. 165), pp. 1268–1269. ◆ Describes the use of a medical x-ray unit to obtain radiographs of the movements of wood-movement clocks. The easily obtained radiographs provide a convenient way of both recording and, particularly the derived contact prints, clearly illustrating the details of construction and operation of this type of clockwork mechanism.

Ternbach, Joseph. "A Sixteenth Century Terra Cotta Statue: Problems of Restoration and Preservation," *Curator*, II:3 (1959), pp. 219–232.

NOTE

Organ Clearing House, P.O. Box 104, Harrisville, New Hampshire 03450. The Organ Clearing House was founded to facilitate the relocation of used tracker action pipe organs which might otherwise be discarded. The Clearing House maintains a constantly changing list of old organs for sale.

APPENDIX

Periodicals Cited

American Antiquity. 1935, quarterly, membership. Society for American Archaeology, 1703 New Hampshire Avenue, N.W., Washington, D.C. 20009.

The American Archivist. 1938, quarterly, subscription. Society of American Archivists, Judith A. Koucky, Acting Secretary, Bentley Historical Library, University of Michigan, Ann Arbor, Michigan 48105.

American Federation of Arts. Quarterly. 1963–1964, quarterly. American Federation of Arts, 41 East 65th Street, New York, New York 10021.

Antiques. 1922, monthly, subscription. Straight Enterprises, 551 Fifth Avenue, New York, New York 10017.

Applied Optics. 1962, monthly, membership. Optical Society of America, Inc., 2100 Pennsylvania Avenue, Washington, D.C. 20037. ◆ Text in English, French, German or Russian.

Archives of Biochemistry and Biophysics. 1942, monthly, subscription. Academic Press, 111 Fifth Avenue, New York, New York 10003.

Art and Archaeology; The Arts Throughout the Ages. 1914–1934. Archaeological Institute of America, 260 West Broadway, New York, New York 10013. ◆ Has been succeeded by *Archaeology,* 1948, quarterly, subscription.

Art and Archaeology Technical Abstracts. 1955, irreg. (approx. 2/yr.), subscription. Circulation Dept., AATA, c/o New York University, Conservation Center, Institute of Fine Arts, 1 East 78th Street, New York, New York 10021. ◆ Analytical bibliography of the world literature relating to conservation technology. Also includes annotated bibliographies on special subjects. Formerly *IIC Abstracts.*

Art in America. 1913, bimonthly, subscription. Art in America, Inc. 1255 Portland Place, Boulder, Colorado 80302.

Art Journal. 1941, quarterly, subscription. College Art Association of America, 16 East 52nd Street, New York, New York 10022.

Biological Photographic Association. Journal. 1933, quarterly, membership. Biological Photographic Association, Inc., Box 12866, Philadelphia, Pennsylvania 19108. ◆ Dedicated to the science, techniques and applications pertaining to the photography of all things which live or have lived.

British Kinematography. 1936, monthly, membership. British Kinematography, Sound and Television Society, 110–112 Victoria House, Vernon Place, London, WC1, England. Current title: *BKSTS Journal.*

Broadcast Engineering. 1959, monthly, subscription. Intertec Publishing Corporation, 1014 Wyandotte, Kansas City, Missouri 64105.

Bulletin of APT. 1969, quarterly, membership. Association for Preservation Technology, Meredith H. Sykes, Sec.-Treas., Box 2682, Ottawa 4, Ontario, Canada.

Bulletin of the American Institute for Conservation of Historic and Artistic Works. 1960, two issues per year, membership. Subscriptions to: Mrs. Barbara H. Beardsley, Director of Bulletin Subscriptions, Dudley Homestead, Raymond, New Hampshire 03077. ◆ Formerly called *Bulletin of the American Group—IIC;* new title as of vol. 13, no. 2 (1973).

Canadian Conservation Institute Newsletter. 1973, quarterly, free controlled circulation. Canadian Conservation Institute, National Museums of Canada, Ottawa, Ontario, Canada K1A OM8.

Carnegie Magazine: Dedicated to Literature, Science, Art and Music. 1927, monthly (September–June), subscription. Carnegie Institute and Carnegie Library of Pittsburgh, 4400 Forbes Avenue, Pittsburgh, Pennsylvania 15213.

Chemistry. 1927, monthly, membership. American Chemical Society, 1155 16th Street, N.W., Washington, D.C. 20036.

CIBA Review. 1937, quarterly, free controlled circulation. CIBA Chemical and Dye Company, Route 208, Fair Lawn, New Jersey 17410. ◆ Editions in English, French, German and Italian.

Color Engineering. 1963, bimonthly, subscription. Technology Publishing Corp., 825 South Barrington, Los Angeles, California 90049.

Curator. 1958, quarterly, subscription. American Museum of Natural History, 79th Street at Central Park West, New York, New York 10024.

Heating, Piping and Air Conditioning. 1929, monthly, subscription. Reinhold Publishing Corporation, 10 South LaSalle Street, Chicago, Illinois 60603.

Historical Archaeology. 1967, annual, membership. Society for Historical Archaeology, Roderick Sprague, Sec.—Treas., Department of Sociology/Anthropology, University of Idaho, Moscow, Idaho 83843.

History News. 1941, monthly, membership. American Association for State and Local History, 1400 Eighth Avenue South, Nashville, Tennessee 37203.

ICA Newsletter. 1952, two issues per year, membership. Intermuseum Conservation Association, Allen Art Building, Oberlin, Ohio 44074.

ICOM News. 1948, quarterly, membership. International Council of Museums, 6 Rue Miollis, Paris, France.

IIC Abstracts: Abstracts of the Technical Literature on Archaeology and the Fine Arts. International Institute for Conservation of Historic and Artistic Works, 608 Grand Buildings, Trafalgar Square, London WC 2N

5HN, England. ◆ Superseded by Art and Archaeology Technical Abstracts.

IIC News, Supplement to Studies in Conservation. 1960, two issues per year, membership. International Institute for Conservation of Historic and Artistic Works, 608 Grand Buildings, Trafalgar Square, London WC 2N 5HN, England.

Illinois Libraries. 1919, monthly (September–June), free. Illinois State Library, Springfield, Illinois 62706.

Image. Journal of Photography of the George Eastman House. 1952, title and frequency varies, subscription. George Eastman House Associates, 900 East Avenue, Rochester, New York 14607.

Indianapolis Museum of Art. Bulletin. 1911, quarterly, membership. Indianapolis Museum of Art, 1200 West 38th Street, Indianapolis. Indiana 46208. ◆ Formerly Art Association of Indianapolis Bulletin.

Journal of Chemical Education. 1924, monthly, subscription. American Chemical Society, Division of Chemical Education, 441 Lexington Avenue, New York, New York 10017.

The Journal of Micrographics. Vol. 4 (1970–1971), quarterly, subscription. National Microfilm Association, 8728 Colesville Road, Silver Springs, Maryland 20910. ◆ Includes subscription to Micro News Bulletin. Formerly NMA Journal, 1967–1970.

Journal of Paint Technology. 1922, monthly, membership. Federation of Societies for Paint Technology, 1101 Knox Avenue, Easton, Pennsylvania 18042. ◆ Formerly Official Digest.

Journal of Photographic Science. 1953, bimonthly, membership. Royal Photographic Society of Great Britain, 14 South Andley Street, London W1Y 5DP, England.

Journal of World History. 1953–1972, quarterly, subscription. UNIPUB, Box 433, 650 First Avenue, New York, New York 10016. ◆ Ceased publication with Vol. XIV, No. 4 (1972). Superseded, beginning in 1973, by Cultures.

The Laboratory. 1928, quarterly, free. Fisher Scientific Company, 711 Forbes Avenue, Pittsburgh, Pennsylvania 15219.

Library Journal. 1876, semimonthly (September–June), monthly (July–August), subscription. R.R. Bowker Company, 1180 Avenue of the Americas, New York, New York 10036.

The Library Quarterly: A Journal of Investigations and Discussion in the Field of Library Science. 1931, quarterly, subscription. University of Chicago Press, 5801 Ellis Avenue, Chicago, Illinois 60636.

Library Trends. 1952, quarterly, subscription. University of Illinois Press, Subscription Department, Urbana, Illinois 61801.

The Log of Mystic Seaport. 1948, quarterly, membership. Marine Historical Association, Inc., Mystic, Connecticut 06355.

Medical Radiography and Photography. 1925, three issues per year, free. Eastman Kodak Company, 343 State Street, Rochester, New York 14650.

Midwest Museums Conference. American Association of Museums. *Quarterly.* 1941, quarterly, membership. Grand Rapids Public Museum, 54 Jefferson Avenue, S.E., Grand Rapids, Michigan 49502.

Missouri Historical Society. *Bulletin.* 1944, quarterly, subscription. Missouri Historical Society, Jefferson Memorial Building, St. Louis, Missouri, 63112.

Museum. 1948, quarterly, subscription. UNESCO Publications Center, Box 433, New York, New York 10022.

Museum News. 1924, six issues per year, membership. American Association of Museums, 1055 Thomas Jefferson Street, N.W., Suite 428, Washington, D.C. 20007.

Museums Journal. 1901, quarterly, membership. The Museums Association, 87 Charlotte Street, London, W1P 2BX, England.

National Association of Watch and Clock Collectors. *Bulletin.* 1946, bimonthly, subscription. National Association of Watch and Clock Collectors, Box 33, Columbia, Pennsylvania 17512.

New York History. 1919, quarterly, membership. New York State Historical Association, Cooperstown, New York 13326.

Old-Time New England. 1910, quarterly, membership. Society for the Preservation of New England Antiquities, Harrison Gray Otis House, 141 Cambridge Street, Boston, Massachusetts 02114.

Paint Technology. 1936, monthly, subscription. Sawell Publications, Ltd., 4 Ludgate Circus, London EC4, England.

Paper Conservation News. 1973, six issues per year, subscription. H. Wayne Eley and Associates, 15 Broadway, New Haven, Connecticut 06511.

Pennsylvania Library Association. *Bulletin.* 1945, bimonthly, membership. Pennsylvania Library Association, 200 South Craig Street, Pittsburgh, Pennsylvania 15213.

Pesticide Handbook—Entoma. 1948, annual. Entomological Society of America, 4603 Calvert Road, P.O. Box AJ, College Park, Maryland 20740. ◆ Published every year except 1973. 1948–1972, published by the College Science Publishers; beginning 1974, published by Entomological Society.

Photographic Journal. 1853, monthly, membership. The Royal Photographic Society of Great Britain, Maddox House 1, Maddox Street, London W1, England.

Photographic Science and Engineering. 1957, bimonthly, membership. Society of Photographic Scientists and Engineers, Suite 204, 1330 Massachusetts Avenue, N.W., Washington, D.C. 20005.

Picturescope. 1953, quarterly, subscription. New York Public Library, Picture Collections (Room 73), Fifth Avenue at 42nd Street, New York, New York 10018.

Popular Photography. 1937, monthly, subscription. Ziff-Davis Publishing Co., Box 1097, Flushing, New York 11352.

PSA Journal. 1935, monthly, membership. Photographic Society of America, 4704-F North Paulena Street, Chicago, Illinois 60640.

Remembrances of Passaic County. 1926, bimonthly, membership. Passaic County Historical Society, Lambert Castle, Green Mountain Reservation, Paterson, New Jersey 17509.

Restaurator: International Journal for Preservation of Library and Archival Material. 1969, three issues per year, subscription. Restaurator Press, Postbox 96, DK 1004, Copenhagen K, Denmark.

Science and Technology. 1964, irregular. American Astronautical Society, Publications Office, P.O. Box 746, Tarzana, California 91356.

Security World: The Magazine of Professional Security Administration and Practice. 1964, monthly, subscription. Security World Publishing Co., 2639 South La Cienega Boulevard, Los Angeles, California 90034.

Smithsonian. 1970, monthly, subscription. P.O. Box 2606, Greenwich, Connecticut 06830.

Society of Archivists Journal. 1955, semiannual, membership. Society of Archivists, Guildhall Library, Basinghall Street, London, EC2, England.

Society of Motion Picture and Television Engineers. *Journal.* 1916, monthly, membership. Society of Motion Picture and Television Engineers, 9 East 41st Street, New York, New York 10017.

South Atlantic Quarterly. 1902, quarterly, subscription. Duke University Press, Box 6697, College Station, Durham, North Carolina 27708.

Special Libraries. 1910, monthly, subscription. Special Libraries Association, 235 Park Avenue South, New York, New York 10003.

Studies in Conservation. 1952, quarterly, membership or subscription. International Institute for Conservation of Historic and Artistic Works, 608 Grand Buildings, Trafalgar Square, London, WC 2N 5HN, England.

Technology and Conservation. 1976, quarterly, free to qualified persons, subscription to nonqualified persons. The Technology Organization, Inc., 1 Emerson Place, Boston, Massachusetts 02114.

Textile Museum Journal. 1962, annual, membership. The Textile Museum, 2320 S Street, N.W., Washington, D.C. 20008.

UNESCO Bulletin for Libraries. 1947, bimonthly, subscription. UNESCO Publications Center, Box 433, New York, New York 10016.

UNESCO Courier, 1948, monthly, subscription. UNESCO Publications Center, Box 433, New York, New York 10016.

Wilson Library Bulletin. 1914, monthly (September–June), subscription. H.W. Wilson Company, 950 University Avenue, Bronx, New York 10452.

Workshop Notes. 1950–1961, nos. 1–23. Textile Museum, 2320 S Street, N.W., Washington, D.C. 20008. ◆ Superseded by *Textile Museum Journal.*

NOTE

For current information and addresses for specialized organizations and periodicals, consult the following:

Gale Research Company. *Encyclopedia of Associations.* Detroit: 1967–. ◆ Volume 1—National Associations of the United States; Volume 2—Geographic Executive Index; Volume 3—New Association. Current edition, 10th, 1977.

Ulrich's International Periodicals Directory. New York: R. R. Bowker Company, 1932–. 1 vol. ◆ Biennial new editions and supplements issued in alternating years. Current edition, 16th, 1975–76.

Index